SUSPENDED

STATE

NEWFOUNDLAND BEFORE CANADA

SUSPENDED
STATE

NEWFOUNDLAND BEFORE CANADA

GENE LONG

BREAKWATER BOOKS LTD.
100 Water Street
P.O. Box 2188
St. John's, NF
A1C 6E6

Canadian Cataloguing in Publication Data

Long, Gene, 1957–

　　Suspended state

　　(Newfoundland history series ; 9)

　　ISBN 1-55081-144-4

1. Newfoundland – History – 1855–1934.* I. Title.　II. Series.

FC2174.2.L66 1999　　　　971.8'02　　　　C99–950036-8
F1123.L66 1999

Editor: Shannon M. Lewis
Design/Layout: Jonathan Holden
Author Photo: Mary Lynn Bernard
Cover Photo: 1932 Colonial Building Riot (PANL A2-159)
Courtesy of Newfoundland Provincial Archives.
"The Final Breath" music and lyrics by Ron Hynes. Courtesy of Blue
Murder Music/ Sold For A Song/ MCA Music Canada. © 1993
Printed in Canada

 We acknowledge the financial support of the Government of
Canada through the Book Publishing Industry Development
Program (BPIDP) for our publishing activities.

ACKNOWLEDGMENTS

This book has been a long time in the making. Portions of it were contained in a Masters thesis completed at Memorial University in 1992. At that time I received tremendous encouragement and a lot of advice from many people in and around the History Department and Newfoundland archival studies. These included Gerrard Bassler, Melvin Baker, Joan Butler, Skip Fischer, Anne Hart, Jim Hiller, Greg Kealey, Linda Kealey, Rosemary Ommer, Bert Riggs, Shannon Ryan, Bob Sweeny, Linda White, Irene Whitfield, Chris Youe and the staff at the Centre for Newfoundland Studies, and the Provincial Archives of Newfoundland and Labrador.

Others who provided personal support and various forms of intellectual sustenance along the journey from those early days include Matt Adamson, Peter Birt, John Doherty, Angela Drake, Patty Gibson, Jim Goss, Justin Hall, Bill Hynd, Philip Lewis, Brenda O'Brien, Jim Payne, Gail Picco, Rachel Rocco and Ellen Waxman. Special thanks to my wonderful Aunt Aileen Kelly for telling me stories that brought the history to life, and to my brother Jed and sister Valerie for humouring me through the process. Mark Ferguson provided critical last minute production and fact-checking assistance. My grateful acknowledgment is extended to Clyde Rose of Breakwater Books for seeing in this a worthy publishing project and to Shannon and Jonathan for making it all happen on schedule. Finally, my apologies to Ann Decter for all the attendant disruptions and my unending thanks for her generous skill and counsel in acting as my in-house editor and all round anchor of strength.

DEDICATION

In memory of my parents
and to Ann and Rosie

TABLE OF CONTENTS

INTRODUCTION

This could be the final breath
This is life and death
This is hard rock and water
Out here where the wind has turned
And the towers are burning
There is no returning

— Ron Hynes, "The Final Breath"

ON DECEMBER 2ND, 1933, the people of Newfoundland, through their elected representatives, accepted the recommendations of a royal commission to suspend the constitutional authority that had grown up through one hundred years of representative institutions, and to install via the issuing of new Letters Patent from the British Crown a unique, and anomalous political experiment called Commission of Government.

Where did the idea for this scheme come from? Given the complexity and detail of the recommendations contained in the report of the Amulree Royal Commission, it could not have just fallen from the sky. The immediate adoption of the report by the parliaments of Newfoundland and Britain inaugurated a critical interregnum between the Depression and the end of the Second World War and the essential formative experience from which Newfoundlanders decided to vote in favour of joining with Canada. In all the attempts to understand how Joe

Smallwood and his supporters were able to defeat the anti-confederate forces in the late forties, not enough effort has been made to examine the fundamentally related question of how the country got itself into government by commission in the first place.

The continuation of the commission experiment was, after all, the third choice facing the population in the first referendum on June 3rd, 1948. It polled a remarkable 14.3% support, behind 44.5% in favour of a return to responsible government and 41.1% for confederation. The supporters of the commission option controlled the fate of the country and provided the winning difference in the second ballot on July 22nd, when their votes went decidedly toward confederation, giving it a majority of 52.3%. [1] Despite all the polarization of opinion which occurred during the second referendum campaign, the outcome was ultimately determined by those whose first choice was to remain without a democratically elected government of any kind.

The Royal Commission of 1933 was an unprecedented joint undertaking between three governments—Newfoundland, Britain and Canada. Directed and controlled by the British Dominions Office, the Commission was chaired by Lord Amulree (Baron William W. Mackenzie), a Scottish labour peer with a long career of public service as an arbitrator of industrial and other disputes. In addition to having authoured numerous publications and editing several prestigious legal journals in Britain, he served as a cabinet minister in the National government of Ramsay MacDonald in 1930-31. Amulree was joined by two Canadians, one of whom, William Stavert, from Prince Edward Island, was Newfoundland's appointee. Stavert had only resided in Newfoundland a short time as he had been temporarily seconded from the Bank of Montreal to serve as special financial advisor to the Newfoundland government in 1932. The other commissioner, Charles A. Magrath, was a former member of the Canadian parliament for the Northwest Territories and a former chairman of the Ontario Hydro-Electric Power Commission. At the time of his appointment, he was chairman of the Canadian section of the International Joint Commission. [2] Together with the aid of British bureaucrats, this eminent panel produced a report which was introduced in the British House of Commons by Neville Chamberlain, then Chancellor of the Exchequer, as "one of the most remarkable and interesting ever drawn up in the history of the Empire." [3]

The Amulree Report, as it has come to be known, continues to receive mixed reviews. At the time of its publication, with one notable exception, it was widely received as having given voice to a popular call for the introduction of a new form of government. The Royal Commission was originally established as a condition of continued financial support from Britain to help Newfoundland meet debt payments due at the end of 1932. The Commission was given a warrant with deceivingly simple terms of reference: "To examine into the future of Newfoundland and, in particular, to report on the financial situation and prospects therein." [4]

The Newfoundland House of Assembly was called into a special session on November 27th, 1933 to debate the recommendations of the report. Newfoundland's last Prime Minister, the conservative Frederick Alderdice, said he believed that the country's forefathers, who struggled to achieve the privilege of responsible government almost eighty years earlier (following twenty-three years of limited self-rule), would agree, if they had been sitting there that day, that what the country now needed was "a political holiday and a breathing space [for] working out its destiny." [5] Alderdice appealed to the country for support of the Amulree recommendations. He had been elected in June 1932 as leader of the United Newfoundland Party with an overwhelming majority and a Liberal opposition of only two members. His government replaced the despised Liberal regime of Richard Squires, who was literally chased from office following a spectacular riot on the country's parliament at the Colonial Building, and dumped electorally soon after.

In his speech to the assembly, Alderdice made it clear that he was not a great proponent of the principle of democratic government which he described as "a curse instead of a blessing" for Newfoundland. [6] He articulated the more or less latent view of the St. John's merchant class. Ironically, for a leading businessmen, Alderdice's preferred strategy had been to default on the country's debt as the means to overcome a protracted financial crisis, but Britain would not allow such action. Instead he was forced by circumstance and by Amulree's recommendations to return to a promise made in his 1932 election manifesto: that he would investigate the idea of commission government as an alternative to the existing political system. [7]

As has been frequently noted, Alderdice's election pledge contained a promise to submit any proposal to change the country's political system to a referendum, but no such referendum occurred. More significantly, what has generally escaped notice is the fact that the idea of investigating a commission form of government was not an original undertaking by Alderdice, nor was this idea a central issue of the 1932 election campaign. [8] The British government, the Amulree commissioners, Alderdice, the country's merchant elite, and the many others who expressed an outpouring of support in favour of closing down the House of Assembly all came very late in the day to embrace government by commission. The idea had been promoted intermittently since 1925 by William Coaker, the founder and long-time president of the Fishermen's Protective Union (FPU).

In a recent assessment of the career of Joe Smallwood, Ed Roberts, the only person to serve as a cabinet minister with all three Liberal premiers since confederation, suggested that New-foundland's political history in this century cannot be understood without examining the contribution of William Coaker. [9] Despite the relevant truth of this observation, Coaker's most lasting impact remains almost entirely overlooked. Coaker is generally regarded as the visionary leader of fishermen who set out to make a revolution in the early 1900's against the nearly feudal conditions in the country's fishery. In contrast to most labour figures of his time, Coaker was not a socialist, though some of his comrades in the FPU were. He had more in common with the farmer-progressive movements of Western Canada and their appeals for group government and direct democracy, as the course of his political ideas eventually demonstrated. Coaker's failure to achieve lasting benefits for the "toiling masses" of the Newfoundland outports is usually cited as the last great effort to save the country before the onslaught of the Depression. [10]

What has generally been missed in both the treatment of Coaker's career and the collapse of Newfoundland's sovereignty in 1933 is the relationship between the two. When the recommendations of the Amulree report were hurriedly pushed through the Newfoundland assembly, it was Coaker who was the exceptional critic, standing almost alone in resolutely denouncing those responsible as "traitors to the land that bore them." [11] But it was also Coaker who had persuaded Alderdice to include the pledge of investigating commission government in his 1932 election platform, following years of an FPU campaign propagating the merits of a similar scheme. At this historic conjuncture, Coaker assumed the role of a tragic progenitor desperately trying to disown a legacy.

Coaker rejected the proposals recommended by Amulree as differing "materially" from those he had been advocating—which included the election of Newfoundland commissioners—and railed against the anti-democratic "despotism" about to be introduced. He also insisted that any such fundamental change in the constitution of the country should not proceed "without first having the matter submitted to the people." He warned that the tranquility of the country would be endangered as immediate agitation for the repeal of such measures would accompany the undermining of authority and "widespread turmoil and unrest." [12]

The British government, in its behind-the-scenes instructions to Amulree, calculated correctly that such alarmist considerations need not carry the day. Instead, the report built its core proposals on a key assertion of support from the people of Newfoundland:

> That it was essential that the country should be given a rest from politics for a period of years was indeed recognized by the great majority of witnesses who appeared before us. [13]

The Royal Commission held about one hundred formal sittings in St. John's and ten other locations travelling across the country by train. They interviewed two hundred and sixty witnesses and received "a large number of letters and memoranda from all parts of the country." [14]

The failure of the British Empire's oldest colony to weather the battering of its national status and constitutional machinery was in keeping with the political trajectory of other nations at the time. Fascism was emergent in Europe, the fragmentation of England's national political scene was unprecedented, Roosevelt was usurping normal constitutional authority for his New Deal, and R. B. Bennett, that most un-endearing Canadian figure, was paralyzed by his own troubles and unable to aid Newfoundland in its time of need. Although the Canadian banks were successful in securing their pound of flesh through several debilitating years, there were no international financing authorities to rescue embattled national economies or impose policies of structural adjustment.

Mid-way through its fifth century as a location of some prominence in the "New World," Newfoundland was, like all other countries, in a stage of nascent formation as a member of the modern international community. It had not joined the League of Nations nor passed legislation to give effect to the Statute of Westminister, in which it had been named as a signatory of the 1926 Balfour Declaration. [15] Having achieved prominence during the First World War for the notable contributions—and proportionally staggering losses—of its regiment, Newfoundland's relatively independent ship of state was an emblem of its national character. However, there were weaknesses of momentous proportions in the institutional foundations of this state. And when the storm hit, the political ballast did not hold.

The story of the unfolding of these circumstances needs some retelling. While the Amulree report, containing an extensive review of Newfoundland's history and detailed description of its urgent circumstances in all their troubled state in 1933, has been recognized as a watershed historical document, there has been no published account of the *in camera* testimony given in the spring and summer of that year to the Royal Commission. Since 1983, fifty years after the transcribing of these hearings by the Commission's secretary, the record of the interviews and the complete papers of the Commission have been available in public archival collections. These papers were, until their release, the property of the Canadian government. They had been deposited in Ottawa as government records in the name of Charles Magrath, the Canadian appointee. The contents of these documents provide an extremely rich mine of information and open numerous windows for further inquiry and reflection. They offer a palpable taste of the old world that was Newfoundland at this time and especially St. John's, the centre of the country's continuous struggle to secure a berth of self-respect against odds that never seemed to show favour. [16]

As James Hiller observed in the introduction to the recently published debates of the Newfoundland National Convention of 1946-48, the history of twentieth century Newfoundland is dominated by "two linked events: the suspension of responsible government in 1934, and the country's decision to join the Canadian federation in 1948-49." [17] The events leading to confederation with Canada are well illuminated in the collected documents and debates, particularly those which focus attention on the drama of that moment as played out by the leading political figures in their own words. Regrettably, no comparable publishing project has brought together or sufficiently examined the records of the first dominant event of the century. The 1933 debates of the Newfoundland House of Assembly, which record the voluntary surrender of self-government, have never been properly assembled. And the literature on the period has almost exclusively concentrated on diplomatic records at the expense of the rich and resonant voices of Newfoundlanders, amply accessible in a variety of primary sources. [18]

In the absence of a thorough rendering of the calamitous circumstances leading to the country's bankruptcy during the Great Depression, one which puts the actions and aspirations of Newfoundlanders themselves in the picture, it is perhaps not surprising that the nature of the linkage between this event and the subsequent struggle over confederation has not been adequately assessed or explained. As a result, Michael Harrington, a long-time editor of the *Evening Telegram*, is able to contribute a personal memoir to the two-volume national convention debates from his point of view as an elected delegate who became an anti-confederate, in which he states, "Indubitably, Newfoundland on the eve of confederation with Canada was still a distinct society, a Dominion of the British Commonwealth and Empire, albeit with suspended status." [19]

That Newfoundland was, and is, a distinct society is not in doubt. But it is something of a romantic fantasy, one commonly invoked by those who opposed confederation, to imagine that at the time of joining Canada, Newfoundland's status resembled that of a sovereign Dominion. Dominion status—bestowed by the 1931 Statute of Westminister—and all accompanying constitutional rights and prerogatives had been lost, or given up, in December of 1933. The significance of this historical fact was established both by the Supreme Court of

Newfoundland in ruling on an appeal against the legitimacy of the Terms of Union with Canada in 1949, and again, more recently, by the Supreme Court of Canada during the offshore jurisdictional battles with Ottawa in the early 1980's. [20]

This "nationalist" view of the tumultuous confederation struggle is partially understandable as an echo reverbating in the minds of patriotic warriors from a viciously fought campaign within living memory. It is also a reminder that historical memory is fickle, and subject to inaccuracy, especially when it involves the failure of a nation. It is no consolation to those who maintain that joining Canada was a sell-out of Newfoundland's birthright, a treacherous foreclosure on the promise of re-establishing national honour and pride, to suggest that the deed was done fifteen years earlier. It was then, during a period of protracted crisis, that the patriotic defenders of the country's good name were not able or so inclined to save the nation from humiliation.

It is arguably not possible to re-construct the profoundly divisive issue of confederation in a meaningful way without revisiting its precursor event with greater care than has thus far been the case. This exercise is not without limitations. As with Newfoundland's fabled oral traditions, alive with their own line of social and political narrative, the story of the end of the nation is subject to change and re-interpretation. While each new account is shaped by and builds on previous versions, the political history of Newfoundland remains a contested terrain. No doubt this is a function of the continuing relevance, and perhaps burden, of the past. The broad history is at once well recorded from many angles, and yet replete with significant gaps and unanswered questions. The work which follows represents an attempt at opening the record for further illumination by applying the tools of revision and synthesis. It is modestly guided by the principle that our history should be made useful in that same unending struggle to move forward which got the better of us in the early, dirty thirties.

PRELUDE TO CRISIS

IN THE FALL of 1925, William Coaker addressed delegates to the annual convention of the Fishermen's Protective Union (FPU) for the last time as president of the organization. [1] It had been a year and a half since the election of a merchant-dominated party, led by Walter Monroe, the self-described "plain man of business," a cousin and business partner of Frederick Alderdice, to whom his leadership eventually passed. [2] In his address, Coaker denounced what he called a "highwayman's administration," one doomed to be "destroyed" by the hostility toward it throughout the country. The partisan tone was typical of the proceedings at FPU conventions, but on this occasion, the president's speech contained a dramatic proposal which went beyond the normal parameters. Coaker called for the formation of a party that would appeal to the electorate on a single issue: "passing a law to place the government in the hands of nine men for ten years, electing the nine men somewhat on the (denominational) lines pursued for years of selecting the Executive (Cabinet)." [3]

Eight years later, in the spring of 1933, Walter Monroe appeared before the Amulree Royal Commission and testified that he "heard it said that the people generally were sick of politics and would like nothing better than a form of commission government for ten years." [4] He added he was doubtful whether this was really the case, and thought public opinion should be tested with a party formed on such a programme and a general election held on the question. Monroe was perhaps being disingenuous in ascribing to others support for an idea which had come to represent the favoured political option of most of the merchant elite, for whom he spoke. But in advocating almost exactly what Coaker had proposed earlier, Monroe's testimony embodied the general "desideratum" of the country identified by the Amulree report. [5]

Much of what has been written about the Amulree report emphasizes that its political recommendations were a cover to allow Britain to convert the bonds owing on Newfoundland's debt to a lower rate of interest, effectively engineering a form of default through receivership. This bit of managerial finesse was, in the British view, preferable to the alternative of Newfoundland taking unilateral action as an independent sovereign, consequently threatening both its own credit and that of the whole British empire. The Amulree report stressed that there was a "twofold character" to any remedy for Newfoundland's situation, one part financial and the other political. [6] While it was self-evident that an unmistakable economic crisis was in full swing, the Commissioners had to go to some lengths to justify the drastic measures proposed on the political side.

Critics have taken objection to those passages of the report which stand as an indictment of the country's political "machine," said to be marked by "a continuing process of greed, graft and corruption which has left few classes of the community untouched by its insidious influences." This claim was attributed to evidence tendered "from all sides and from responsible persons in all walks of life." [7] It has been argued that many of these witnesses were caught up in the whirlwind of troubled times and as a result scapegoated and exaggerated with impunity in their supplicating deference before the British lord. [8] It has also been noted, and this is both more relevant and more true, that the evils of Newfoundland's political system were not unique and the mature bureaucratic model of British governance was an inappropriate and unfair standard for comparison. [9]

HISTORICAL ANTECEDENTS

THERE IS AMPLE evidence in the historical literature demonstrating that the collapse which was already in motion during the proceedings of the Amulree Commission came as a result of economic and not political factors. The most coherently argued of this material shows that the country's difficulties arose not as a result of "a riot of spending by corrupt politicians," but rather from a historically driven tendency to "replicate the economic performance of its continental neighbours" by importing development strategies unsuited to Newfoundland's very narrow economic base. [10] In addition, the failure of successive governments during the 1920's to properly regulate the country's fishery produced "a steady march toward stagnation and dependence," a process notable for its contrast with Iceland and Norway who were winning the competition for European markets after the First World War. [11]

On the other hand, all the correct economic analysis does not adequately address the troubling reality that the country, in addition to losing its credit, had lost all sense of political efficacy. The much repeated view that Newfoundland had an honourable case for default in its own right, was first put forward by a group of prominent Canadians, including Harold Innis, in 1937. [12] But, it was not the collapse in the price of fish in 1930, nor the violence which grew from the desperation of the poor, nor even the appearance on the scene of interlopers sent by the Mother country, that precipitated a general crisis of self-confidence in the country's ability to govern itself. The enormously despondent loss of faith which produced a largely grateful embrace of anti-democratic measures had numerous antecedents.

The Amulree report noted "there was almost unanimous agreement among witnesses that the present period of misfortune might be regarded as having originated" with the defeat of Robert Bond as Prime Minister by Edward Morris in 1908. [13] Allowing for some hyperbole in the attribution of opinion, this note nevertheless signals a historical depth in the self-conscious articulation by intervenors of the problems facing the country. Elsewhere the Commission presented a view counterposed to the one it heard: "We ourselves would have been inclined to place the commencement of this process [of deterioration] at an earlier date." [14] It expressed sympathy with the view of the island's leading historian, Judge D. W. Prowse who in 1895, a year after the failure of Newfoundland's two banking institutions, offered a severe critique of a political system in which "merchants and politicians on both sides have helped to bring the unfortunate Colony into disrepute by the fierce rancour and bitter personal hate which characterized their party struggles." [15]

Though the country's collapse was not inevitable, for most of the nineteenth century Newfoundland's political history was characterized by features of inherent weakness and instability. The granting of a representative assembly in 1832, which gave way to full responsible self-government in 1855, may have established a lasting national base for the aspirations of middle class reformers. But there was also an overriding sectarianism between Catholics and Protestants that served as a dangerous driving force behind political behaviour. Following the St. John's riot of 1861

that saw three people killed and twenty injured, a permanent constitutional convention—the "denominational
principle"—was adopted as a method for achieving representative executive councils and for the distribution
of public works. [16] The three main religious groupings,
Catholic, Methodist and Church of England, were to be
equally represented in the conduct of all the affairs of
state. It has been argued, a case that is also made in the
Amulree report, that this principle, which nominally put
an end to sectarian strife, actually institutionalized "the
pervasion of sectarian politics through the whole of public
life." [17]

It may be, as S. J. R. Noel observed, that this unusual
framework converted the merchant Protestant elite to
reluctant acceptance of the "evils" of liberal democracy. [18]
But if this was a basis on which responsible government
was given a relatively secure lease, it was not long before
its tenure was tested as the first great debate concerning
confederation with Canada came to dominate the later
half of the 1860's. Perhaps most interesting in this struggle
was not the arguments in favour of joining the Canadian
project, but the nature of the alliance of those opposed.
Irish Catholics, who resisted confederation with Canada as
a threat to "Home Rule," joined with Protestant merchants, whose interests were vulnerable to Canadian competition. As James Hiller noted:

> The anti-confederate party emerged as a strange coali-
> tion of left and right, those espousing the maintenance
> of responsible government on principle, and those who
> hated responsible government but had to argue for its
> maintenance from a belief that confederation would
> bring catastrophe. [19]

Having rejected the supporting recommendations from the two delegates who attended the 1864 Quebec conference, Newfoundland voters eventually defeated the pro-confederate party when it campaigned on this issue. In so doing, the country would seem to have established some measure of self-confidence in pursuing an independent destiny. However, the foundation was fragile. Surveying the thirty-year period following the election of 1869, Noel described the workings of the political system, a description which prefigures the post-1908 decline:

> Thereafter there was little to distinguish one party from another. Parties, in so far as they may be said to have existed at all, were mere ad hoc creations, cabals of politicians whose association with one another signified nothing more than their common desire to capture the government. And each government in turn stood on a quicksand of shifting alliances within the Assembly, where the real struggle for power took place.... Elections gave the people a choice, went a popular aphorism, "between merchants and lawyers and lawyers and merchants." [20]

The last years of this era saw the trauma of the great fire of 1892, which destroyed a third of the city of St. John's, and the bank crash of 1894, which the Amulree report described as having "a far-reaching effect on the Island's political economy." [21] A new set of confederation negotiations were undertaken with Canada to seek favourable terms that would restore Newfoundland's credit following the failure of the local banks. The negotiations failed and a threatening financial crisis was avoided through the extraordinary initiative of Robert Bond who, as Newfoundland's Colonial Secretary, offered his personal savings as collateral and negotiated a private loan in

London to save the country from insolvency. [22] Financial stability was achieved by the arrival of three Canadian banks, the first of which, the Bank of Nova Scotia, was established by none other than William Stavert, later appointed as Newfoundland's representative to the Amulree Commission. [23] With the election in 1900 of Bond, the last Prime Minister remembered fondly by the witnesses in 1933, the country reached the short-lived zenith of its maturation.

What is perhaps most interesting about Bond's tenure, from the perspective of later events, is that it was framed by two fundamental challenges to the exercise of the country's sovereignty. The first was the infamous 1898 Reid railway contract, which forced a division in the country on a question of basic principle: "Whether the government or a private industrial empire was to be the greatest power in the land…the ancient battle over responsible government flared up again." [24] Bond's opposition to the deal provided the basis for a near sweep by his Liberal party in the 1900 general election. Elected as an ardent patriot determined to defend the country's integrity, this eventually became his greatest political liability.

Bond's insistence on carrying forward the struggle for Newfoundland's independence, following a successful campaign to win possession of the French Shore in 1904, brought him into an extended conflict with Britain, the United States and Canada over U.S. fishing rights in Newfoundland waters. [25] In the end, Bond lost not only the immediate battle to the combined forces weighed against him, but also his standing in the country, which was finally undermined in the election of 1908. This did not happen by a clear vote against his Liberal party, but rather a tie election was resolved by the colonial Governor of the day in favour of Bond's opponent, Edward Morris.

Morris, who along with Michael Cashin, had resigned from Bond's government for essentially opportunistic reasons, contested the election under a new People's party which brought together all the elements of the anti-Bond opposition. [26] Bond's fall from grace thus reflected a diminution in Newfoundland's ability to function in the larger world and the deepening of personal animosity as a motivating political principle. It was also marked by an injudicious interference in Newfoundland's affairs through the authority of the Crown's representative (a source of constitutional conflict elsewhere, as Canada would come to experience in the King-Byng affair of 1926).

THE COMMISSION IMPRINT

IN THE FIRST years of the century, Newfoundland's proverbial ship of state was battered, but on the face of it not beaten. However, it was not long before its carrying capacity would be put to much greater strain. The years which saw the birth of the Fishermen's Protective Union, followed by the First World War and its aftermath, also produced a number of important features in the collective experience which warrant reference in situating this period in a longer view. These include: the administration of the war effort; the tenuous position of the municipal government in St. John's; the political orientation of the working class; and finally, the failed efforts of William Coaker to introduce state regulation of the fishery in 1919.

The first two issues bring into focus aspects of the administration of government that would later reverberate in the proposition that the very function of representative institutions could perhaps be a dispensable part of public life. As it did for others, the war left a defining mark on Newfoundland's slowly maturing sovereignty. The lasting damage was apparent not only in the permanently debilitating cost of servicing debts incurred to the treasury, but, as recorded by David MacFarlane and others, in the effect of massive and ultimately unquantifiable losses to family and community. [27] Following the logic of military imperative, the administration of Newfoundland's contribution to the war involved the virtual disappearance of civil authority. Collusion between Prime Minister Edward Morris and the British Governor in directing the activities of the National Patriotic Association (NPA) produced a mode of operation characterized by "disregard for the constitutional conventions of responsible government," which according to one study of the period, "did not worry anyone as long as the war effort enjoyed the support of the three political parties and major opinion leaders." [28]

There are various subsidiary issues here, including the recurrence of extraordinary conduct by a governor and the shameless profiteering of Water Street merchants which resulted in legislation limiting the ability of the Assembly's upper house, the Legislative Council, to act on their behalf. The experience of conscription was critical, as was William Coaker's decision, as a minister in an all-party national government (and leader of a group of nine FPU elected members), to sanction its introduction over the profound objections of his supporters. For many fishing communities, conscription marked the end of Coaker's unchallenged authority to speak for their interests. Throughout this period there was also a continuing effort by Morris, the Reid Company and others to promote confederation. [29] But perhaps the most significant development was in the function of the Newfoundland Patriotic

Association, in the creation of a parallel public authority which existed outside and beyond the normal political framework. What began as an undertaking to construct a broad consensus amid an uncertain base of popular support for the war was eventually institutionalized through the formation of a national government. Party politics were first subsumed by the overriding dictates of organization, and then, transformed out of this into a parliament without opposition. These were the cornerstones of an idea, an imprint of the commission model, that would reappear later at another time of national reckoning.

During the war, the city of St. John's experienced a comparable case of administrative authority substituting for elected representation. As the result of an initiative by merchants concerned about increasing insurance costs owing to inadequate water supply and fire protection services, and of confusion arising from overlapping jurisdiction with the legislature in setting local tax rates, a special commission was appointed in 1914 which governed the city for two years. This commission had a mandate, among other things, to prepare a charter which would clarify the legislative basis of municipal government. Because of delays in granting approval for this charter, the mandate of the council elected in 1916 on an interim basis was extended by the legislature annually until 1920. At this time, a second commission was appointed to govern the city while arrangements were made to hold the first election under the new charter. Further delays caused the replacement of this commission by yet another, following an interim period of a month when the city was without a governing structure of any kind. [30] This extended absence of any municipal electoral process over four years may have popularized notions about reconciling representation with the need for sound administration. This theme found constant expression in concerns about the country as a whole in the decade which followed, even among those who were not advocating a wider application of a commission form of government.

SMELLING THE BRIMSTONE

THE WAR PERIOD also generated dramatic changes in class relations. There was a tremendous mobilization of strength by the industrial working class of St. John's which, while corresponding with similar movements throughout the world, is in part significant because it did not connect in any meaningful way with Coaker and the FPU. From the inception and dramatic growth of the FPU in 1908, and through its successive electoral campaigns, first in an alliance with Bond in 1913 (winning nine of ten seats contested) and then Squires in 1919 (winning eleven of twelve), the fishermen's union had not built or sustained links to either Catholic communities or St. John's workers. The opposition of the Catholic church was a potent reactionary force as it set out to stem the secularizing influence of self-organization among the people. This dynamic has been well-documented as a countervailing factor in limiting the reach of the FPU. [31]

Less recognized is the extent to which Coaker as leader was responsible for the alienation of the union from those parts of the country where it never took root. Early on, he took steps to diminish the union's practice of rituals associated with the Orange Lodge, but his ongoing insistence on campaigning for prohibition reinforced the appearance of the union as dedicated to Protestant ideals. As for St. John's, Coaker laid out a view at the union's founding convention in which there was little to distinguish the workers there from their employers:

> Our aim is to benefit the country, as well as the fishermen, while the unions at St. John's exist to secure advantages for themselves at the expense of the fish catchers in the outports. Theirs is for self, which of course is their right, ours is a noble endeavour. [32]

In addition to his efforts to fight high import tariffs, which were supported by the city's workers but caused price increases for fishermen, Coaker's links to the Reid family during the war made him suspect in the eyes of militant railway workers when they staged a massive and successful strike in 1918 against the Reid Company. [33]

Eventually, Coaker's antipathy towards the interests of the city's working class had direct political consequences. The Newfoundland Industrial Workers Association sponsored candidates in the election of 1919 with the deliberate purpose of offering an alternative to the FPU as a general representative of the country's workers. [34] Coaker's approach to politics, aside from his less-than-forthcoming disavowal of any "socialistic tendencies" in the union, [35] was from the outset complicated, and arguably compromised, by both a "balance of power" strategy in seeking leverage rather than government, and also by his emphasis on building the FPU as a co-operative commercial enterprise, and ensuring the Union Trading Company was imbued with "the adoption of business principles." [36] In any event, it did not take long before the independent entry into the political field by St. John's labour became co-opted in an alliance with the city's merchants in the name of combined opposition to the Liberal-FPU government of Richard Squires.

Which brings us to Coaker's fishery regulations of 1919. The essential outline of what transpired between November of that year, when Coaker's initiative as the new fisheries minister was introduced only days after the election of Squires' government, and January 1921, when the regulations were withdrawn, is detailed elsewhere. [37] In short, the regulations were designed to achieve stability in European fish prices, particularly in the Italian market, by setting minimum prices that exporters were obliged to follow. They were also to achieve quality control by issuing licences with rules governing inspection and standardization. A single government agent taking direction from an Exporters' Advisory Board was appointed to negotiate the sale of all fish to the European markets. The *Daily News*, one of two opposition papers in the capital, began a virulent campaign against the programme and gave over its pages to relentless invective toward Coaker, who it insisted was in conflict of interest as minister and head of the union's trading company.

The regulations had the full support of the Board of Trade and all the chief exporters, notably John Crosbie who, as Minister of Shipping in the short-lived Michael Cashin government at the end of the war, had been working to implement similar measures. But during the fall trade season, there was a group of recalcitrant merchants led by A.E. Hickman who broke ranks and sold cargoes of fish on their own terms in defiance of the regulations. This "sensational development" was hailed by the *Daily News* as a decisive breakthrough, and the regulations were effectively suspended by the Board of Trade upon a recommendation of the Advisory Board on January 6, 1921. [38] Coaker was in Europe at the time supervising the implementation of the scheme and was powerless to arrest its unravelling.

While this episode has been recognized for its historic display of merchant myopia, in the inability of the "Trade" to follow a disciplined course designed to safeguard its own interests, there was another critical result. On his return from Europe, Coaker filed a number of articles with the union's paper, the *Evening Advocate*, in which he defended the regulations and denounced the actions of Hickman and the "political clique" of Crosbie, Cashin and the *News*. He also went further and drew on the experience as an indication of the desperate state of politics, "where evil is deep rooted and far exceeding what is generally believed." [39] He signalled his own disillusionment and confessed that he no longer had a desire "to remain a public man." One month later, when the House of Assembly opened and Coaker had to speak to a *pro forma* withdrawal of the regulations, he took up a theme which he had invoked during the bitter struggle, pleading for politics to be set aside in the national interest, lest the country's independence be threatened:

> I say again it is time to place country first and party any-where. The question of the country comes first and all other considerations must follow that. What I want done is that which is best for the country, and I will do all in my power to assist in bringing that about. If we persist in only debating while unemployment is increasing and fishermen are without supplies, we are hastening the day when confederation will be staring us in the face. [40]

Coaker's advocacy of a non-partisan approach to the main challenges facing the country was a refrain familiar from the days of the national government. It also revealed his disenchantment with the uneasy alliance he had undertaken by joining forces with Squires. [41] In addition, there was an ambiguity in Coaker's relations with the fish merchants, whom he courted as one-among-them while seeking their co-operation with the regulations. On the one hand, he was determined to pursue a course in politics and commerce as an independent agent with a relatively clear set of objectives. At the same time, as a once-feared union leader who had become a member of the country's elite (having been knighted for his recruitment efforts during the war), he was treading a path fraught with contradictions.

A year later, at the FPU convention of 1922, Coaker openly indicated his dissatisfaction with Squires by announcing his intention to resign from politics because he was convinced he could exercise more influence outside the Executive Council than in it. He reflected on his political experience and described it as the vilest of business: "The life of a public man nowaday is one that few should envy, it is as near Hell one can go without smelling the brimstone." [42] His plan to leave politics was, however, soon overtaken by a fascination with the promise of industrial diversification represented by the Humber pulp and paper project in Corner Brook. [43] To demonstrate his support for this development, he again contested the election of 1923 alongside the victorious Squires, and subsequently found himself surrounded by a scandal which produced the most bizarre events yet witnessed in the political life of the country, summarized by Noel:

> Politicians of all parties engaged in a wild scramble for office, scarcely moving outside the capital for fear of missing their place in the game of musical chairs. The scene was one of unprecedented confusion. Factions

mysteriously took shape and just as mysteriously evaporated; the puzzling combinations of one day became the bitter feuds of the next, and vice versa. Party politics became meaningless; the party system, such as it was had evaporated. [44]

Between July 1st, 1923 and July 1st, 1924, five different administrations held office. Squires was forced to resign by a revolt of four of his ministers, including William Halfyard, the senior FPU member, who demanded answers to allegations being made in the opposition papers. These included that Squires was responsible for widespread diversion of public funds to his own account and accounts of his supporters. A caretaker government was then formed by William Warren which appointed an inquiry under the direction of a British civil servant. (Coaker had declined to sit in Squires' cabinet after the election, but accepted a position from Warren without portfolio.) The head of the inquiry, Thomas Hollis Walker, reported in March 1924 with a damning indictment of criminal behaviour on the part of Squires and Dr. Alex Campbell, his Minister of Agriculture. The full text of the report, and the lengthy proceedings which gave rise to it, were widely published and showed Squires as an unconscionably corrupt first minister who had misappropriated funds for his personal benefit on a massive scale. He had arranged and supervised his own kickbacks from the liquor distribution system and the similar diversion of monies earmarked for relief projects for his re-election campaign. [45]

When Prime Minister Warren signalled his intention to prosecute Squires and to extend the investigation to other government departments, his administration was brought down by an extraordinary intrigue—which evidently arose from collusion between Squires and a number of opposition members, including Michael Cashin—to limit the damage to only those so far implicated. [46] Squires, arrested and out on bail when the House was called, managed to induce four members of the government to break rank and vote with the opposition on a measure of non-confidence. Squires himself cast the deciding vote. Warren then formed a second government by jettisoning Coaker and the FPU and making his own alliance with the opposition. This effort soon failed and when Coaker declined an invitation to form a government, he recommended A.E. Hickman, the exporter who had played the lead role in breaking his fishery regulations. [47] Hickman then led a party called "Liberal-Progressive" into an election against a party which had come together around businessman Walter Monroe calling itself "Liberal-Conservative." The election gave the appearance of party lines being hopelessly confused, as in part they were, but in Monroe's campaign focus on the evils of "Coakerism"—a catch-all pejorative meant to invoke the meddling hand of an anti-business regime—at a time when Coaker was not a candidate, there was a clear expression of the new government's loyalty to the merchant class. [48]

Walter Monroe's election returned the country to a point where political conflict could be seen to reflect real ideological differences, and these would manifest before long. But in the meantime, there had been a relentless series of assaults on the integrity of the political system and the character of most of those who participated in it, with the notable exception of the FPU members. Squires was never prosecuted, and the various incarnations of the Liberal party were scattered in many directions. The fall-out from the revelations of the Hollis Walker inquiry would resonate for some time to come. Widespread revulsion in the face of a massive spectacle of corruption and self-interest provided the essential point of departure for the floating of an idea reflecting what most people knew to be true: the institutional foundations of the country's public life were weak, vulnerable to abuse, and not demonstrably capable of meeting the country's promise as a self-confident community. In this fog of political despondency, William Coaker appeared with a beacon for those seeking a new way forward.

HISTORY CLOSING IN

IN SEPTEMBER 1924, as part of an FPU re-organization, the union's weekly newspaper, now called *The Fisherman's Advocate*, moved its operations from St. John's to Port Union, the home of the Union Trading Company and site of the FPU annual conventions. John Scammell, a long time member of the House of Assembly, was appointed editor. [1] Announcing its new mission, the paper promised it would henceforth be "free-lance" and not tied to any government. It had moved from the capital to escape what it called dominating influences, which "touch almost every hem of the political garment, whether government or opposition, and [where] the truth is often half told or absolutely concealed because the wheels within wheels operating in St. John's are powerful enough to coat almost any crime with sugar." [2]

While the FPU was adjusting to its politicians being back in opposition and its president out of politics and focusing on commercial activities, Coaker was again tempted into an active role in the political game. He decided to contest a by-election in his old seat of Bonavista, won by Monroe in the general election and which the Prime Minister had then to re-contest, according to an anachronistic law governing the remuneration of members of the Executive Council. [3]

In Coaker's decision to run in this by-election—which produced the only electoral defeat of his career—his personal moral convictions took precedence over his political judgement. It is clear from an appeal made by Hickman, leader of the opposition, to recruit him as a candidate, and from Coaker's own analysis after the event, that his primary motivation was to campaign against the Monroe government's swift repeal of prohibition laws. [4] Coaker's determination to invest in an issue which represented no serious challenge to the new government shows the extent of his deeply held moral views and his willingness to bring these into sectarian politics, such that his campaign relied almost entirely on winning the support of Methodist voters. No doubt he was also driven by a sense of obligation to ensure a semblance of debate in providing a voice of opposition to the Prime Minister, even if it meant being alone on an issue which otherwise had generated an "overwhelming consensus." [5] It might also be that Coaker was unable to resist the call of partisanship himself, despite his professed view of the decline of principle in public life.

In 1925 a second by-election, or rather the absence of one, became a focus of attention for Coaker and provided the context for his speech to the FPU convention in the fall, where he introduced the proposal for government by commission. Early in August, the Liberals led a delegation to Governor William Allardyce and presented a petition requesting his intervention to fill a vacancy which had existed for six months in the district of St. John's East. The governor responded according to advice given him by Monroe's cabinet. He forwarded a letter to Hickman, outlining the constitutional implications of the request and stating that he had no authority to act, as such responsibility lay entirely with the government. [6] The government was stalling to wait out a heavy backlash resulting from an income tax reform that had been transparently designed to benefit merchants—including the Prime Minister and other members of his cabinet—at the expense of the general population. The resignation from the government over this issue by the young (Major) Peter Cashin provided the opposition with an obvious issue, one which was magnified as the government refused to call the by-election. Cashin had inherited the seat of Ferryland from his father in 1924, from whom he had also evidently learned the fine art of resigning with fanfare. [7]

The *Advocate*, as the country's only national opposition paper, seized on the issue of the delay and commenced a fierce campaign of hostility directed towards Governor Allardyce. [8] The paper also focused its attack on A. B. Morine, an irrepressible figure whose shadow was behind various political plots for thirty years (dating from the Reid railway contract) and who, as the government leader in the upper house and a member of the cabinet, publicly justified the by-election delay, drawing attention to himself as a lead strategist behind Monroe. [9] The *Advocate* accused the governor of driving a nail into "the loyal feeling" of the people toward the Crown. The tenor of the editorial commentary contained more than the usual flair for overstatement:

> We feel sure that thousands of the people, who are sick and disgusted with the farce of governments that has existed during the past twenty years, and who find each party securing power turning out much worse than their predecessors, will view with alarm and indignation the action of the Governor, in proclaiming himself as the tool of the Tory party, the butchers of our constitution, and the upholder of an alien imposter in his usurped position as a dictator of Newfoundland. The governor must be recalled. He no longer possesses the confidence of all the people of this country. He has become a part of the Tory machine, and there are men in this country

who will die before tamely submitting to such ignominy and outrage. [10]

As the *Advocate* developed its campaign against the governor, it returned to a curious and unsubstantiated suggestion that support for annexation by the United States was growing as a result of the government's refusal to call the by-election. Editorials warned that if a plebiscite were to be held, support for joining with the US "would exceed two thirds of the votes cast." [11] The notion of annexation may have resulted here from frustration with the limitations of British parliamentary institutions, but this represented the beginning of a search for alternatives to the existing political order and an expression of interest in exploring all possibilities.

An East End Electors Committee, formed to mobilize support in the city, soon organized a public meeting and demonstration described by the *Advocate* as "one of the largest and most representative ever witnessed in St. John's." [12] Having been denied entry to the governor's residence, the demonstration "marched around the town to the accompaniment of three bands, with skyrockets and fireworks of every description." This was followed by an address from Michael Cashin, who although retired from politics, Coaker believed was likely to be the opposition candidate. [13] In a letter sent to the British Secretary of State for Dominion Affairs seeking guidance on the issue, Governor Allardyce said that the crowd had nearly been incited to violence by Cashin's speech, from which he quoted as having been delivered after the parade left the governor's residence: "If those present had the spirit of their forefathers the gates would have been pounded down and there would have been a wreck at Government House." [14]

The morning after this show of strength, a petition of six thousand names was presented to the governor. Allardyce did his best to assure the deputation that he had no wish to act "other than in a constitutional way" and suggested they give further consideration to the matter and to his position. [15] During the following weeks, the governor requested but did not receive further direction from the British government, and wrote again to the Secretary of State, this time seeking advice on whether he should file an action against the *Advocate* for libel. He reported that senior ministers, including John Crosbie, were urging him to do so and that he had received the support of the Prime Minister should he proceed. But despite what he called a campaign of "scurrility and abuse," he felt it would be difficult to obtain a conviction from a local jury, in view of the failure of the prosecution against Squires for corruption in the wake of the Hollis Walker inquiry. In favour of legal action there was a benefit to be derived in "cleansing the political and public life of the Colony." [16] The British Secretary of State replied that it was up to the governor whether to proceed, but he should not go forward without "definite and formal advice from Ministers to do so." [17] No such action was taken, but a deepening political conflict was clearly under way.

SUPPLIES FOR THE FUTURE ARCHITECT

THIS VERY PARTISAN campaign against the governor provided the most recognizable feature of Coaker's speech at the end of November to the 1925 annual convention of the FPU in Port Union. These assemblies represented the only continuous extra-parliamentary forum in the country, and were a significant outlet for democratic debate, even though the hundred or so delegates from the union's predominantly northern districts were towered over by the force of the president's oratory and personality. Unlike the dramatic call for a commission form of government contained in the same speech, the campaign against the governor received immediate support from the delegates. In contrast, the commission idea was not automatically endorsed in the normal routine manner in which the president's proposals were received. It was, however, not inconsistent with the attacks against the governor. Together, the two issues involved a general calling into question of constitutional precepts. Coaker's remarks focused on Allardyce's conduct and suggested a nominee to replace the governor. He said he had been "pressed by scores of correspondents to make the selection of a governor a live issue and petition the Home Government to appoint Sir Robert Bond the next governor." He went on to offer a general warning to his listeners:

> If this is not done there can be no protection in future for public rights and privileges from governors, and in defense of the rights won nearly ninety years ago by the Fathers of Responsible Government. [18]

Coaker evidently saw no contradiction between his proposal for a commission government and those rights and privileges of responsible government which he held to be sacrosanct.

Coaker immediately followed up the request to focus on the recall of the governor and the appointment of Bond, but was determined to put his own mark on this campaign. In the next edition of the *Advocate*, which contained a text of his speech, he published a letter to the paper's readers and attached a ballot containing three questions. The first question asked whether the governor should be recalled by the King. The second whether the King should be asked to appoint Sir Robert Bond as governor, and the third was: "Are you prepared to support candidates pledged to pass a law to have the country's public affairs administered for ten years by an elected commission as outlined in my recent address to the FPU convention?" [19] The incongruity between the first two and third questions is apparent in Coaker's description of these issues as "matters of lively importance," on which he was seeking guidance. Except for his own convenience, it is difficult to see how the question on commission, which had no previous public airing, could be taken as a "lively" issue. [20] In addition, Coaker described the proposed measures as designed to give the people "a greater control and voice in the government of the country." This may have been true of the first two questions, but it is not at all clear that the application of the third would have met such a test.

Coaker was in fact launching a tendentious initiative behind an already dubious campaign in which constitutional authority was challenged by a weak argument concerning the position of the governor. There is no doubt that Coaker and his colleagues successfully generated a hostile sentiment towards the office of the Crown's representative, but this was in large measure fuelled by a classic partisan attack originating in the by-election delay. It is significant in this context that alongside Coaker's questionnaire, the *Advocate* ran two editorials, one in reference to the three questions and another reviewing the FPU convention. Neither endorsed nor even directly addressed the commission of government idea. The first editorial dealt only with the governor, and said people were questioning the value of the office as they were satisfied he had broken the law and had become a "tool" of Morine, the government's strategist. On the convention, the editorial obliquely suggested Coaker had presented proposals on "far-reaching subjects" which had been received enthusiastically and were considered "easily adjustable to present day requirements." Thus, his speech had "given a lead to thinking men." This contrasted to a specific note that resolutions on the governor's recall and the appointment of Bond were carried unanimously. [21]

In its next edition, the *Advocate* reported on the first results of what it called "our referendum" and in response to these, began to flesh out the commission idea, putting forward a number of qualifications and expressing reservations about its practicability. It reported that all the replies received, with one exception, had been in favour of all three questions. An editorial explained that a commission was an alternative that would likely have to be faced in four or five years and only then because it would be preferable to "Government by Downing St. or Government as a province of Canada." In a second editorial, the paper called Coaker's proposal a warning which had rendered "a signal service" if it had done nothing more than to set people thinking. It admitted that not everyone would "see eye to eye with Sir William," and cautioned that his views represented opinions and not "positive dogmas." Such a tentative review in a paper which otherwise stood fast by everything Coaker said and did represents both the extent to which Coaker was staking out ground entirely on his own and also the reluctance of his colleagues to follow what was seen as a radical course. In a final note the paper insisted that Coaker was "actuated by the highest motives" and concluded with an observation of remarkable prescience:

> If his views are not at all times feasible and his plans capable of practical application, he at least supplies the future architect with the essential and basic idea of the new structure. [22]

This is precisely what would transpire eight years later with the issuing of the Amulree report.

In the meantime letters from readers were starting to pour in. The *Advocate* reported that hundreds of forms were being received daily and that the "greatest surprise" was the support for the third question advocating commission government. This was taken as evidence that people seemed to have been thinking seriously about "some alternative form of State management other than that of the Party," and one of the reasons for this was that they were "staggered" by having A. B. Morine dictating the policy of the country. It also noted that it was "not pleasant" to observe the amount of disrespect toward the governor, but this could also be explained by the "nauseating aspect" of his conduct in following Morine's advice. [23]

In a series of columns published over the next two months, sample letters were published containing a variety of approaches and points of view toward the three questions. These tended to represent a simple affirmative on all three, in deference to the request of the president, but demonstrating no high degree of commitment to or understanding of the specific proposition of commission government. This is hardly surprising. The program was basically an ambiguous one which, while advocating the abolition of party politics, was at the same time characterized by partisan rhetoric and repeated calls, by both Coaker and the *Advocate*, for the defeat of the government and its replacement at the next election by the Liberal Party.

This inherent tension was illustrated in Coaker's New Year's message. He rejected appeals that he re-enter politics to lead the Liberal party, and instead called for a united opposition to defeat Monroe and to advance a policy of establishing a commission form of government. [24] This would have obligated the new government to immediately call another election, one which, according to the proposal, would be organized along denominational lines. In effect, party politics would be replaced by sectarian representation. Both the method of electing the commissioners and the constitutional basis of such an election represented two great "practical" problems—previously referred to by the *Advocate*—which would return to haunt Coaker in 1933.

On this occasion at the start of 1926, Coaker explicitly emphasized that the basis for his prescribed program was an impending crisis that would herald an appointment with destiny:

> The day is not far distant when the country will be forced to decide, probably with its back to the wall, whether it will be governed by a commission elected by the people, by the nominees of the British government governing as a Crown Colony, or as a poverty-stricken, Godforsaken province of Canada.

In this he was not only accurately anticipating the prospects that would be confronted by the Amulree Commission, but was also setting in motion an irrevocable process of defining the options in advance and submitting his own pre-disposed preference. If history was about to close in, Coaker was determined to try and give it shape, rather than have the country molded by inexorable circumstance. The *Advocate* took a more optimistic view, one that more clearly reflected partisan objectives. It saw "a day not far distant when once again Liberal principles will rule in government, [and] Liberal institutions [will be] safe from Tory marauders. [25]

The difficulty of reconciling immediate political goals with more fundamental reform was apparent in many of the published responses from readers. In one letter, an "Observer" in Eastport had given the proposal for a commission government "much consideration" and came to the conclusion that the government was "a bunch of bluffers and should be banished." [26] For many of the correspondents this clearly did not mean the banishment of party politics per se, as in the view of a Trinity resident who expressed agreement with the president, but took this to mean that "Liberals like Bond, Coaker and Hickman should replace Monroe." Others seemed to support the commission on the expectation that Bond or Coaker would lead it. Some did, however, address the proposal on its own terms. One of the first letters printed was from a writer in Port Union who was struck by the idea, having concluded "for some time past that some drastic change from our present system of government is necessary." [27] Another, from Corner Brook, suggested that ten years would be too long and that maybe a commission would not be necessary if Coaker would return and lead a government that "could and would do what a commission would do." [28]

Many of the letters complained that more copies of the *Advocate* were not available in their communities, or said that in lieu of this they were writing on behalf of others. On the 8th of January, barely one month after the publication of the questionnaire, the paper reported it had received "about three thousand" replies, and again, on the

22nd of January, stated that forms were still pouring in. If this can be taken at face value, even with some allowance for exaggeration, it indicates that Coaker had indeed succeeded in creating a live issue. [29] But the nature of what had been brought to life is not entirely clear. Amid a growing constitutional conflict, he had planted a seed wrapped within a partisan campaign to promote an idiosyncratic idea, one which, as he predicted, would only emerge in full form when the country found its back to the wall.

THE RETURN TO LIBERALISM

WHATEVER THE EXTENT of informed support for Coaker's commission proposal, the effort to foment opposition to Monroe's government had an immediate impact. As pressure continued to have a writ issued for the overdue by-election, Coaker refrained from promoting the commission idea beyond his original intervention and pushed for mobilizing other political energies. He approached the East End committee on the by-election issue with an offer to co-ordinate a petition campaign outside St. John's. [30] He then appealed to local FPU councils to prepare for the possibility of a general election and to circulate petitions for the re-call of the governor and the appointment of Bond as a means of maintaining a high level of "political interest." [31] That he did not mention the commission issue suggests it would have distracted from a more straightforward appeal to partisan activity, already moving forward on a number of fronts.

Coaker received a report from Ken Brown, a labour lea- der and Liberal member of the House from Grand Falls, informing him of a recent conversation with Peter Cashin, now sitting as an independent member. Cashin had indicated that he did not like the idea of a commission running the country, but was "apparently right out for a Squires-Coaker-Cashin combination" as the means to defeat Monroe. [32] The formation of exactly this coalition would eventually lead a successful assault on the government, but it would be some time before this could be put in place. The first break in the political scene appeared in the form of an open cleavage created in the spring of 1926 by the resignations of no less than five members of the government, including Gordon Bradley, who would figure prominently in the events of 1933 as leader of the Liberal opposition. [33] The coming together of the coalition referred to by Cashin occurred as a consequence of the death of his father Michael, the intended candidate for the by-election which still had not been called.

Upon the death of the senior Cashin, Coaker, after publishing a warm tribute to his old enemy, inquired of Peter's political intentions. Cashin responded by expressing a keen interest as a "young public man" in taking advantage of any advice Coaker had to offer, in view of a political atmosphere which necessitated "the various chiefs" giving careful consideration to their respective positions. [34] Shortly thereafter, Cashin wrote a second time. He complained about the approach being taken by Liberal leader Hickman in preparing for two imminent by-elections which had been called outside St. John's and his lack of commitment in pressing the issue of St. John's East, where a by-election had still not been held. [35] These preliminary exchanges were expanded several months later when Cashin responded to an inquiry from Coaker about "political rumours" of attempts by Monroe, to construct a coalition government out of his precarious position in the House. Cashin confirmed there was "plotting" underway to dump Monroe and intrigues being planned by various players to attempt a coalition with the opposition. Cashin assured Coaker that he would not be party to such manoeuvres: "The Standard Manufacturing Company could not manufacture sufficient soap to wash me clean if I again become associated with them." [36] Cashin was continuing his dialogue with Coaker while giving the appearance of being disinterested in the ongoing permutations around him.

When the two by-elections outside the capital were held in November 1926, returning one government and one opposition member, the results provided the only point of reference for Coaker's commission idea since earlier that year. Commenting on a low voter turnout, the *Advocate* suggested that people were sick of party government and would vote two to one in favour of government by commission for a period of eight or ten years as "the only hope of sane administration of public affairs." [37] At the end of the year Coaker's annual message contained no mention of commission, but emphasized the need for fishery reform and predicted Monroe was likely to "smash" in the spring, resulting in a big Liberal victory. The *Advocate*'s year-end editorial re-stated the view that people were sick of Monroe and of "all governments in general," but did not refer to the commission idea. [38] In January the paper returned to this theme in a reflection on "the country's position," and stated that "politically, the people are in a wilderness." It said the country was without a government, except in name, and referred to "wild men" outside the government who were acting as "clowns of the lowest calibre" and dictating policy. [39]

The political plots which Cashin described to Coaker soon became the subject of open speculation. If accounts in the *Advocate* were correct, this activity represented a bizarre twist on the commission idea, as the government appeared to borrow from it in an attempt to save its own life. The paper accused Monroe of planning to appoint a Royal Commission to "overhaul the general condition of the colony's affairs and to give it an unlimited period to conduct its work." [40] Details of a strange series of events were published a month later, giving evidence of Monroe's attempts to entice members of the opposition to join with the government in forming an administration that would resemble the national government of the war years. The *Advocate* was then in the curious position of having to denounce what it called "persistent talk" of government by commission indulged in by members of the government, without making any distinction between such scheming and the idea it had been trumpeting. [41] Sub- sequently, any discussion of commission was dispensed with as the by-election was finally called in St. John's East and the government suffered a major defeat in what had been one of its strongholds. This result was, of course, proclaimed as a return to Liberalism.

BURYING MISGIVINGS

THE ADVOCATE REMAINED silent on the idea of government by commission until the end of 1927, when it ran an editorial on "Democracy" in which it reviewed an address on the topic by Sir Edward Grey, British Foreign Secretary during the war. In an inconclusive and ambivalent summary of Grey's remarks concerning the need to defend democratic institutions, the editorial noted that the validity of these institutions was being questioned both at home and abroad, and, referring to its own campaign for commission government, suggested the friends of democracy could take solace in Grey's views. [42] The same tone carried over into the paper's review of the FPU convention, in which no mention was made of any need for constitutional changes, but rather the people were said to be anxious for an opportunity at the next election "to efface political hypocrisy from their midst." The perennial issue of fishery reform was emphasized, along with the need for governments to follow the wishes of the people in order for the whole "system of government not to be subverted." This would ensure that Newfoundland would not be forced to "strike her flag as a self-supporting, progressive Commonwealth." [43]

It would appear there was no longer a deliberate campaign to promote the commission idea, as partisan imperatives were once again ascendent. Coaker concentrated on the re-organization of the Liberal party and the re-entry on the scene of Richard Squires. The first public indication of this work seemed to appear out of nowhere when Squires emerged to dissociate the Liberal party from an alleged move by the government to open talks with Canada on confederation. In a published letter, Squires signed himself as Liberal leader, and in so doing made a frontal assault on Hickman, who evidently had not shown enough electoral promise to satisfy Liberal back-room brokers. Among these, if his own account can be believed, was the young Joe Smallwood. [44]

When the House of Assembly reopened in May, nine members of the opposition, including seven unionists, with William Halfyard as their spokesman, announced they had formed a new Liberal party with Squires as their leader. Peter Cashin was not a member of this group and explained that his non-alignment was because "local political parties are so much nonsense...There is not a member of this House who has not been on either side at one time or another, who has not been either Liberal or Tory." [45] This of course was not entirely true, as the elected FPU members generally remained in their place and as such constituted the only coherent political formation over a long period, despite their association with the Liberal party. Notwithstanding his disclaimer, Cashin was clearly a part of this move against Hickman as he eventually signed on with Squires and Coaker to create the formidable coalition he had envisioned three years earlier.

The Liberals were not the only group re-organizing in anticipation of a general election. In July, Monroe resigned and turned over the office of Prime Minister to his cousin and business associate, Frederick Alderdice. Like Monroe in 1924, Alderdice came into office as a merchant without any political experience. Both men were Protestants born in the north of Ireland. The October election saw the return of Coaker alongside the victorious Squires, as once again the FPU brought its strength to the aid of the Liberal party. That Coaker and Cashin (who both took up senior Cabinet positions, Coaker without portfolio and Cashin as Minister of Finance) were prepared to bury any misgivings about Squires says something of their desperate desire to bring about a change of regime. Unfortunately, the decision to rehabilitate a figure who they correctly calculated could win the support of the country, in the end did not deliver the desired dividends, and instead caused no end of regret to both these men and the whole country.

There was no discussion of government by commission during this campaign. Coaker was determined to make another attempt to reform the fishery and focused on advancing the Liberal cause in traditional unionist terms:

"The experience of the past four years has convinced every fair minded man and woman that Tory rule is class rule." [46] It is worth noting Coaker's reference here to women voters, as this was the first general election in which women had a limited franchise, with eligibility at age twenty-five compared to twenty-one for men. [47] During the campaign Coaker held a meeting in Bonavista with "about three hundred lady voters" which the *Advocate* described as "the first women's political meeting held in Newfoundland by a candidate to consider the issues of a general election." [48]

Another development of note from Monroe's term was the succesful reference in 1927 to the Privy Council in London of a longstanding dispute with Quebec over the Labrador boundary. Newfoundland's ownership claim was confirmed, providing a significant boost to the prospects and general morale of the country. A short while later, facing the financial squeeze brought on by the Depression, Newfoundland attempted to bargain away this prized asset. It was hoped that Canada would make an offer to enter serious discussions on the property, estimated by Newfoundland to a value in the range of $100 million, an amount not coincidentally representing the country's total accumulated debt, against which its future was mortgaged. [49]

THE COUP OF '32

THE FRAGILITY OF the resurrected alliance between Coaker and Squires was almost immediately apparent as Coaker returned to his public disavowal of the system of party government. Within months of taking office, Coaker wrote to the FPU councils and expressed his concern about the declining strength of the union and the lack of active participation among its members. He was especially distressed by what he saw as a "spirit of self-seeking and self-interest" overtaking the principles of co-operation and unity. In a revealing passage, he confessed alarm at what he found upon re-entering the government:

> I am shocked at the spirit which is coming over our people. Everyone is after a government job. Members tell me they are deluged with applications for jobs of one sort or another. I have about 150 applications for jobs myself. When we fought the election last Fall we fought it on a fishery policy, and better and brighter industrial and social conditions in the country generally. We believed that we won our election on that platform. Apparently it was not so, for now everyone writes for jobs and favours. Few, if any, ever write their member about a fishery policy or industrial development or ask in what way and when we intend making a move to improve conditions. No one writes us on such public issues as these. Great issues seem to have been submerged beneath the self-seeking that is everywhere so prevalent. [1]

If Coaker was shocked by the behaviour of his own supporters, he could hardly have been impressed with the game of politics as it continued to be played, inside and outside of parliament, while he struggled to formulate a new set of regulations to reform the fishery. In April 1929, the *Advocate* offered another in its periodic reflections on the political scene and asked: "Is everybody a hypocrite? Are all our public men hypocrites or simply politicians, or what?" The paper suggested the country's progress was cursed by politics and political considerations, particularly when it came to the fishery, and called for the opposition and merchants to dispense with partisan activities and get on with "patriotic action by all those qualified by experience." [2] Coaker was once again consulting with Water Street merchants to prepare a new programme for the grading and export of fish, which would be presented in legislative form in 1930. In the summer of 1929, increasing unemployment, particularly in St. John's, also became a focus of concern as the *Advocate* urged the government to be careful in its approach so as not to "saddle" the whole country with the burden of providing relief for the city's workers. [3]

The combined effect of these matters brought Coaker to a renewed sense of despair by the end of the year. In his annual review of the general situation, he referred to his address of 1925 and the proposal for commission government, and wrote that he was "more convinced than ever of the soundness of my contention." Coaker admitted he did not know whether the country would "tolerate such a change" but thought the people should be given an opportunity to express an opinion on the matter. He revised the numbers for the commission and called for the election of six men. Although he was assuming only men would be elected, he emphasized that "care must be exercised by the women voters and an effort to get back to political sanity made through their efforts." He complained of the strain politicians were under to respond to the constant demands on the treasury from all sides, and concluded that the "necessary changes to political sanity" could not be brought about under the existing system of electing party governments, "be they Liberal or Tory or Labour." He ended on a note that would be sounded again and again through 1933, and in the pages of the Amulree report, when he observed that there was a time when politicians who offered money to voters would "destroy the temper politically, but today the bribing politician is the most sought after and the most popular for a period." [4] Because of the expectation that politicians would go to extremes for votes, it now seemed they had little to do other than deliver on their promises of patronage and spoils.

On this occasion, Coaker's comments were taken up by both the *Daily News* and the *Evening Telegram*, the country's two anti-Liberal papers. The *Telegram* headlined its commentary, "Coaker's Faith Destroyed" and noted that he "had abandoned the last vestige of hope" that the country could administer its own affairs. The paper gave him credit for showing "frankness and courage" in leaving himself open to charges of "infidelity to his own colleagues." It said that while his criticism of party government reflected on the administration of which he was a part and was, therefore, "extraordinary," his views were "very much to the point." It added:

> Not a few are beginning to wonder whether it is not actually the case that we have ceased to show ourselves capable of managing our own affairs, and whether it would not be a wise plan, even though it would be a

> humiliating admission of incapacity, to ask for the sus-
> pension of our constitution, and for the appointment of
> a commission with power to administer the affairs of the
> Colony until such time as political sanity had been
> restored. [5]

This expression of interest in Coaker's proposal indicates
the success of his promotional efforts over a period of several years. But, in describing the commission as appointed
and not elected, the editorial illustrates that even at this
stage the idea was misunderstood and misrepresented on
what, for Coaker at least, was a critical and defining issue.

The *Daily News*, in contrast, showed no sympathy
whatsoever and used the occasion to launch a broadside
against both Coaker and the government. It said Coaker
was evidently "tormented by a pricking conscience" and
described the proposal as calling for "a sort of dictatorship—of which he would, of course, like to be a part." The
News charged that Coaker did not believe what he said
about one party being no better than another, which was
probably true, and accused him of attempting to hide his
own cowardice in not being forthcoming about matters
"that would shake the administration to its very foundations." Coaker's "utterances" could not be sincere or taken
seriously, it argued, when he was failing in his own responsibilities by rarely attending Cabinet meetings as he "had
not been in the city a dozen times" in the past year. [6] The
News demonstrated, as it always had, the finer points of
partisan realities and confirmed the risks Coaker ran in
speaking openly from what was clearly an untenable position for a minister. In 1928 Coaker had arranged to purchase land in Jamaica, where he now spent most of his
winters, enjoying the beneficial effects of the climate on a
serious bronchial condition. [7]

Throughout 1930 Coaker focused on a renewed attempt at fishery reform. By the end of the year, he believed that the legislation he had presented in the spring would be successful in establishing the necessary regulatory "machinery." This explains his continuing presence in the government ranks. But his hope for reform was clearly tempered by an exasperation resulting from twenty years fighting on the issue. As he saw it, "a system to standardize salt fish and regulate its export is more, in my opinion, than Party or Party government." In these year-end remarks, he went on to reflect on his comments of a year earlier, which he noted had "caused considerable conversation, especially among politicians." Coaker said that being one year older, he was "more convinced than ever" that his commission proposal was in the best interest of the country. [8]

The *News* responded to Coaker's message by suggesting that it differed from that of the previous year by focusing on the fishery and described the content as "an admission of his own impotence." [9] The paper was essentially correct. Coaker was revisiting a bind from his battle of ten years earlier with the exporters. And the issues were exactly the same, as he struggled to devise rules for a form of self-regulation to which all would agree. In the face of opposition from west coast exporters who held influence with Squires as the member representing Corner Brook, Coaker eventually proposed exemptions in the scheme for non-participants, which only served to undermine the purpose of any such legislation. [10]

BACKS AGAINST THE DEBT WALL

IN THE SPRING of 1931 sustained opposition began to be mobilized against the government. A committee of St.

John's merchants issued a call for a royal commission to address the country's growing financial problems. As the depression deepened, a collapse in fish prices combined with dramatic increases in relief expenditure to create an ever-expanding deficit on the current account. The government faced an immediate crisis in meeting interest payments on outstanding loans—due twice a year on the 1st of July and the 1st of January—and in finding creditors to negotiate new loans. [11] In early July, to stress the urgency of the situation, and re-open discussion on options the country might have to consider, the *Advocate* reprinted the text of Coaker's 1925 speech. It was at this time, in accordance with stringent conditions laid out by a syndicate of banks in return for fresh loans, that the government launched a systematic attempt to cut expenditures. Coaker assumed the duties of directing retrenchment.

According to the *Advocate*, Coaker was applying a knife "assiduously" in the interest of "national stability and advancement," for which the country would be forever grateful. This assertion was accompanied by a historical review of the propensity by successive governments for overspending, which criticised the two Squires' regimes as "not one whit less blameless than the Tory administrations preceding." In a subsequent edition the paper promised that when the next election came it would "campaign for men of merit and not party." It said Coaker would not stand at the next election and would not be connected with any party, as both the Liberal and Tory parties had men in their ranks who "should never again presume to seek public support." [12]

The most significant event in the fall of 1931 would appear to have occurred in England, where traditional party politics turned inside out to make way for Ramsay

MacDonald's National Government. Led by the leader of the Labour Party, who was disowned by most of his followers, the government was largely an amalgam of Tories and Liberals brought together to see Britain through its own financial troubles. This had an immediate impact in Newfoundland as it provided a model for dealing with an intractable financial crisis. Before long, Squires was reported to be making overtures to the opposition, as a result of a free hand given him by members of his government. The *Advocate* now appealed for a "country first" policy and for the opposition to forget "self and party" and to "shoulder their portion of public responsibility." [13] Such advice was not likely to be heeded, particularly when it carried the familiar ring of similar appeals made in the dying days of the Monroe government.

Calls for the formation of a national government were now being alternated with a return to the issue of commission as *Advocate* editorials insisted the people were "fed up with the game of politics." The paper predicted that "if a true and tried leader" appeared on the scene advocating placing the country in the hands of "a small commission for ten years," he would sweep the country. [14] In December 1931, it reported that people were widely discussing the commission idea and in response to requests from "several correspondents," presented a detailed outline of how the proposal would work, stating the essential features as previously put forward by Coaker. The paper suggested that a national government be formed to extend the existing parliament so that it could prepare a law for the suspension of the Elections Act and then sponsor an election of six commissioners. It further expressed the view that confederation was not an option unless terms were "extremely generous," suggesting this was not likely as

Canada had turned down an offer on the purchase of Labrador. [15]

The financial position of the country continued to deteriorate. Another deadline for loan repayment fell due at the beginning of 1932. The government was forced to accept an ultimatum from the banks which placed extra-ordinary restrictions on policy making, amounting to a virtual receivership. [16] These conditions had a direct impact on the government's ability to respond to growing demands for work and relief. The announcement of a reduction in relief rations provoked immediate agitation in St. John's. The House of Assembly opened on February 4th, 1932 with a portentous speech by Peter Cashin, who had resigned three days earlier as Finance Minister (having faithfully served in that position since 1928). Cashin accused the Prime Minister of falsifying minutes of Cabinet to conceal fees he had been paying himself out of public funds, including an annual sum of $5,000 from the War Reparations Commission. A week later, Squires was assaulted at his office in the Court House building by several hundred unemployed workers organized as a self-styled Citizens Committee. Various accounts of this event emphasized that the "crowd," which the *Advocate* estimated at about 1200, were left waiting in the February cold for several hours while the Prime Minister met with his cabinet. The building was nearly ransacked and Squires, who received several cuts from flying glass, escaped serious injury by guaranteeing that dole provisions at the previous level would immediately be made available. [17]

During the next few weeks, the financial situation worsened. The government prepared further cuts in spending while attempting to float new loan issues. In the wake of Cashin's allegations the political atmosphere was

G E N E   L O N G

approaching a point of no return. The two opposition papers in the city were scathing and unrelenting in their indictment of Squires. The charges levelled by Cashin instantly triggered a widespread view that the government was finished. The allegations of misappropriation—a second time around—were one thing, but the brazenness of Squires in continuing to stymie the efforts of the opposition to launch an investigation under the rules of the House produced unqualified outrage. Alderdice had proposed a motion to appoint a committee of inquiry, but Squires himself amended this to have the Governor review only the specific issue of whether minutes had been falsified. When the governor reported that he had not been "deceived," but supplied copies of minutes and agenda items which showed obvious discrepancies, the uproar intensified. Private charges were brought by a member of the opposition against Squires, who was also the Justice Minister, and against Alex Campbell, an infamous accomplice previously exposed by Hollis Walker. Campbell, a minister without portfolio, was receiving payments as an immigration officer, even though there were no such duties, and had not filed income tax for several years. Three members of the government resigned, including cabinet minister Harris Mosdell, when new taxes on foodstuffs were announced and the pensions of war veterans reduced. Two others followed, including P. J. Lewis, another member of cabinet who confirmed publicly that the minutes of meetings he had attended were indeed falsified. Coaker was not in the country at this time but returned at the end of March to witness an explosion. [18]

THE PURSUIT OF SQUIRES

THE MERCHANTS WHO had organized public meetings against the government a year earlier, now directed their energy toward an unprecedented demonstration of gathering public sentiment. A public meeting was called for Monday night, April 4th, to adopt a resolution for presentation to the House of Assembly calling for a "full, final and conclusive inquiry" into the charges made by Cashin. This meeting, which went on for four hours and featured "over sixty citizens" on stage, was held in front of a packed hall of about 1,500 people at the Majestic Theatre, with an overflow crowd hooked up by speaker at the Longshoreman's Hall and broadcast to the city on radio. Led by members of the merchants' Citizens Committee (the unemployed held no monopoly on this moniker), the meeting was turned over to a variety of speakers, and featured several incendiary addresses, including one by a Rev. W .E. Godfrey. Introducing the resolution, Godfrey said that the people had a "solemn, undeniable" right to know whether the charges were true, a right that "in almost any other country, would be to court riot and bloodshed in a determination to find out."

Gordon Ask, described by the *Telegram* as a "well-known citizen," made the obvious point: "Politicians can rob thousands of dollars and get away with it, but if the common man stole a flour barrel it meant he had to go to jail." Ask suggested all constitutional steps should be taken, but "if it has to be a revolution, let it be a revolution." A war veteran, J. H. Adams, spoke directly to his comrades in the audience and said that if an officer on the battlefield had been accused of "misdeamanours of such a serious character," and was found guilty, he "would stand before a firing squad and be shot." No one needed reminding that the Prime Minister was accused of stealing from funds that were an entitlement of the veterans. The resolution was adopted unanimously and notice given of a "parade" that would take place the next day to petition the Assembly. A motion was passed to send copies of the resolution to every outport newspaper in the country. The meeting closed with the singing of the national anthem to the accompaniment of the Guards band.

The next morning's edition of the *Daily News* carried a front page advertisement from the Citizens Committee addressed to the "employers of the city" asking that leave be given to all employees who "desired to take part" in the afternoon's parade. The paper contained a detailed account of the previous night's meeting and an extensive excerpt from a speech given in the Assembly the day before by Peter Cashin. Cashin said he wanted to "cut the mask of hypocrisy from the faces of the Prime Minister and those associated with him." After re-stating the immediate outstanding charges for what he said was the benefit of Sir William Coaker, who had not been present during their previous airing, Cashin proceeded to level new allegations of bribery and corruption relating to the 1928 election. He accused Squires of having illegally imported two hundred cases of scotch whiskey from a Montreal distiller and accepting donations of $15,000 toward his campaign in return for promises of future business. For Cashin, the worst part of the "scotch orphans" story—one he admitted was widely rumoured but he had not revealed for four years—was that Squires did not make any "earnest endeavours" to return the favour to the distillers. Instead Squires tried to pass himself off to the electorate as a prohibitionist while secretly campaigning with illegal liquor.

Screaming headlines of yet more scandalous revelations likely persuaded additional numbers to leave their workplaces and join the day's parade.

The population of St. John's at the time was about 40,000 people. [19] If the crowd count in the *Evening Telegram*—between 8,000 and 10,000—was correct, then virtually every adult male in the city was in attendance. Existing film footage shows a foggy day and a massive crowd, led by the Guards band and the Union Jack, making its way through the winding downtown streets on its way to the Colonial Building. [20] Most of the faces are men, although a large gathering of women and youth waited on the grounds of the legislature. Anticipating the crowd was also a squad of about thirty police, including four on horseback. Arriving for the public opening of the House at three thirty, the Citizens Committee sent a delegation to the Bar of the House seeking to have the prayer of its petition acknowledged. A procedural argument ensued, during which the Speaker declined to accept a motion of referral to committee from Squires, as the Prime Minister himself was the subject of the petition. Just as agreement to establish such a committee was reached, a disruption occurred in the gallery and all hell began to break loose. Stones rained in through the windows in all directions.

The delegation retreated to the front of the building and called for the parade to re-assemble and return to the Majestic theatre. A sizeable portion of the crowd evidently left the grounds. Those who stayed, apparently numbering about three thousand, began an assault on the locked front doors, behind which was the squad of police. A classic case of misjudgement followed, as the police "divested themselves of their greatcoats" and launched a baton charge on the front steps. They smashed heads "left and right" and momentarily succeeded in clearing the front of the building.

Unfortunately, their colleagues on horseback had no such luck. "Like a flame, a desire for revenge took possesion of the crowd," according to the *Telegram* report. "There were no leaders but the crowd appeared to divide into sections to prevent the exit of the police and the executive heads of the government." Two of the mounted police were pulled from their horses and sent to hospital with serious injuries. Entry to the legislature was gained through the side door basement and pandemonium followed as most of the building was trashed. Fires were set, and the police and others barricaded the Speaker's chamber where Squires and a group of supporters were holding out.

While Cashin and a number of clergymen, including the Reverend Godfrey, tried to restore order, the crowd sent forward a delegation of about forty men who entered the building. They returned with Squires through the front door and proceeded to escort him through the grounds to a waiting car. The crowd had other ideas. Night was falling and the situation was extremely tense. For an hour the escort made its way across the couple hundred yards to Military Road in front of the grounds and onto Colonial Street. From there the Prime Minister was "by some manoevering," according to the *Telegram*, put into Mrs. Connelly's house at #66, where he was able to exit through the back. Here he jumped a fence, went in through the back of another residence on Bannerman Street and slipped into a waiting vehicle. The people gathered on Colonial Street could not believe he had escaped. They would not relent until a delegation was sent to inspect Mrs. Connelly's house. A slight shower of rain began to disperse the crowd, but it was not until after midnight that the Assembly grounds were vacated. At that point, having lost the pursuit of Squires, liquor stores became the desired prize. Through the night bands of angry men roamed the streets, raiding both downtown liquor stores and smashing shop windows.

The next morning the Great War Veterans Association published a front page notice in the *Daily News* calling all ex-servicemen, and other citizens, to immediately report for duty in patrolling the city. More scattered looting occurred that day. Over the next several days, the papers reported that more than two thousand men had been sworn in as special police. No doubt some of these special constables were among the many unemployed in the city who would have been pleased to get regular work. Not a few of them would have been at least witnesses to the great riot of Tuesday afternoon. The papers were full of post-mortems and related arguments. Twenty people had been treated for injuries. Squires was said to be in hiding and Coaker was rumoured to have resigned. The committee of the unemployed published an advertisement seeking "the full co-operation of the unemployed in helping to preserve law and order in the city." Alderdice published an appeal to fellow citizens, telling them they "could do no good by force," to "go quietly" to their homes, and offering a guarantee that justice would be done. The opposition would exert all efforts to ensure the resignation of the government.

The head of the constabulary wrote a letter to the *Telegram* stating no order had been given to lead a baton charge. Peter Cashin sent one saying that contrary to rumour spread by the government, he was not behind "mob rule," and was retiring, "temporarily at any rate," from public life. Front-page advertisements taken out by the insurance firm Outerbridge and Daly assured coverage against losses from riot and civil commotion, at "very low rates." And there was great objection taken by correspondents to a cable sent to the outports by a government member claiming that the crowd had been "primed with rum" before demolishing the House of Assembly. In its weekly edition after the smoke had cleared, the *Advocate* ran an editorial under the headline "A warning uttered seven years ago." It claimed there were many men in both parties "who feel strongly that the parliamentary system of government by elected representatives has failed badly in recent years." It also re-printed an excerpt from Coaker's 1925 address calling for a commission government.

HARD WORK AND TONGUE ABILITY

THE RIOT AND civil unrest in the spring of 1932 represented, among other things, a continuing capacity for vigourous political mobilization in the capital city in the face of popular disillusionment and alienation. Sometimes the grievances were narrow and partisan as in the parade of 1925 demanding the issue of a by-election writ. On other occasions, such as the demonstrations of unemployed workers in 1921 or the railway strike of 1918, the motivation was more broadly political and directed toward achieving basic goals of social justice. In 1932, a long tradition of protest reached a climax which can only be seen to have suited the gravity of both the charges against Squires and the material conditions of the period. It also, not incidentally, represented a recurring and historic common purpose between the St. John's merchant elite and the city's poor and working class in opposition to an outport-led Liberal government.

Later that summer, Coaker wrote a series of articles reflecting on his career, including two which focused on the events around the riot. [21] He said that when he heard what was said at the public meeting, had he been Minister of Justice, he would have arrested Rev. Godfrey "for making such utterances which were capable of creating civil commotion amongst the unrestful section of the community." In Coaker's view, when business was closed down the next afternoon, "reasonable precaution and discretion were overstepped," and the conditions were created for excitment and agitation among the "thousands in the city" who were barely existing on food supplied by the public charities department. He was convinced that if the "mob" had gained entry to the Assembly chamber, Squires and others would have been killed. This would have "meant bloodshed all over the country." He went on at some length about the "cursed game" of party politics and said the desperate situation confronting the country "would prove a blessing if the people will wake up and cast away party affiliations in voting and support candidates only for their merit."

In a review of the twenty-year experience of the FPU in politics, Coaker also wrote a curious defense of the disgraced Squires as "the cleverest politician the country has ever produced." [22] He said that "hard work and tongue ability" had made him successful as the only Prime Minister triumphantly returned in three consecutive campaigns. In a what-might- have-been reconstruction of the last year of the government, Coaker wrote of the unpleasantness of retrenchment, of closing railway lines, feeding sixty per cent of the population, finding work for the unemployed of the capital, and making massive reductions in education spending and all other expenditure. He pointed out that Squires dissolved the House for an election only after securing provision for the interest due on the debt in July, and for this and other achievements he deserved credit. He suggested that Squires should have resigned in the summer of 1931 when he could not raise a public loan, and turned the government over to Alderdice or a national administration. He would then have escaped the hostility to further cuts in spending, and the "boot would have been on the other foot." Coaker believed it could have been Alderdice turned out as the "black sheep" and Squires eventually returned as the "man of the hour."

In this, Coaker was of course doing his best to protect his own good name from guilt by association. But these observations, in addition to denying the significance of what had become a career of illegal acts by the Prime Minister, also represent the remarkable staying power of a politician whom Coaker was not alone in defending. It was the legacy of Squires, after all, that Joe Smallwood cited many times as the source of his own inspiration. Buying votes with liquor, dispensing patronage from funds established for relief of the disadvantaged, and paying off friends and supporters with government contracts—these were the features of a model of political gamesmanship in which the authority of public office was routinely undermined by a shameless disregard for minimal standards of morality. The public purse and the people's trust in their democratic institutions were violated again and again as political leaders played fast and loose with the niceties of legal convention. There is a discomforting irony in the image of Coaker taking the lead in highlighting the veritable rot of such a system and, at the same time, defending in the most partisan terms its greatest practitioner.

An Elephant on the
Back of a Cat

HAVING CARRIED OUT the necessary post-riot repairs to
the Colonial Building, Squires mustered enough political
courage and support to recall the House and pass extraordinary legislation granting the terms for a new loan. After
the Canadian banks refused to honour any more credit,
the Imperial Oil Company was induced to buy $1.75 mil-
lion worth of government bonds, the amount necessary to
cover interest payments due in July, in exchange for a
monopoly on the importing of gasoline products. [1] The
government also introduced further spending cuts, and
included in this was a bill to reduce the number of seats
from forty to twenty-seven. The House adjourned with an
election called for June 11th, 1932. The Liberals were dec-
imated, reduced to two seats. Squires did not run in
Corner Brook, but his seat went to Gordon Bradley, who
became Liberal leader. Squires and his wife Helena, the
first woman elected to the legislature in a 1930 by-election, were defeated in Liberal strongholds. All but one of
the twelve FPU seats fell to Alderdice's United
Newfoundland Party, as incumbent members declined to
stand. Harris Mosdell, who resigned from Squires' cabinet
after the riot, was elected as an independent. [2] As in 1928,
when Monroe was defeated, the only real issue of the campaign was getting rid of a discredited regime.

Contrary to standard accounts, Alderdice's party was
not elected with a mandate to implement government by
commission. Despite the best efforts of Coaker and the

Advocate, commission was at best a peripheral issue, though Coaker did succeed in persuading Alderdice to include the promise of an inquiry into its feasibility as an addendum to his ten-point platform. [3] The *Daily News* commented on Alderdice's pledge, noting that "for some time expressions of opinion" had been heard that some form of government by commission should be adopted until the country's finances had been rehabilitated. Such opinion, it said, may not have been generally held among the people, "but it was one not infrequently offered as a solution for our economic difficulties." [4] That the idea originated with Coaker, as Alderdice publicly acknowledged, and that it was directed in the first place toward political reform, went without notice.

The *Telegram* addressed Alderdice's programme without referring to this promise of an inquiry, emphasizing instead the "solemn pledge" to conduct the country's affairs in an "honest, efficient, economical and business-like way." The explicit implication was that this was a pledge Squires "could not possibly give," and the only way the country could "be given its chance" was by returning to sound principles of administration. [5] The *Advocate* expressed dismay during the election that the commission idea was not being promoted: "What is strange about this pledge of the Opposition Leader is that very few of his candidates have referred to the matter from the public platform." As a result, the paper once again reviewed Coaker's proposal in detail, with the increasingly familiar warning that the country faced the greatest crisis in its history and would within two years be forced to choose between confederation, default on its interest payments, or government by commission. [6]

In editorials that read as if written by Coaker himself, the *Advocate* continued to revise the scheme for implementing the commission idea, and suggested a referendum be held with sixty per cent approval required. In its discussion of an election for the suggested six commissioners— two Anglican, two Methodist and two Catholic—the paper acknowledged there might be some difficulty in selecting the right men, but said they would be no worse than any other six "that for a quarter century has sat at the council table." There was no recognition of the problems that would be created by denominational representation in areas with unclear majorities, or of the lack of representation for substantial minorities. In its last edition before the election, the paper suggested thousands would not bother voting who would "gladly sweat to get to the polling booths if government by commission were an immediate issue." [7]

From these accounts it is clear that the commission proposal was not a central concern of the election. Alderdice agreed to adopt the promise of an inquiry in an attempt to appeal to those voters who did not normally vote for a merchant's party but who, as readers of the *Fishermen's Advocate*, would respond to an idea clearly identified with their leader. It may be that Alderdice had personally come to view Coaker's idea positively, particularly insofar as it converged with a merchant sentiment that responsible government was dispensable in any event. There is no evidence, however, that at this time either he or other leading forces outside the FPU were committed to such a radical proposition. While the proposal for commission government had received some attention over a number of years, its active circulation was largely within the limited purview of Coaker and his supporters.

SURRENDER IN PROGRESS

FOLLOWING THE JUNE election of 1932, the economic crisis in the country deepened. There were major public disturbances, including riots in St. John's in July and Conception Bay in the fall, as the unemployed continued to organize against cuts to relief spending. [8] By the end of 1932, Alderdice's government was out of options. It could not meet loan payments without submitting to new and more restrictive limits on its scope of action. This time the creditors were not the banks, but the Canadian and British governments. They advanced new loans to prevent a default threatened by Alderdice, with the stipulation that a joint commission of inquiry would be appointed by all three countries, and the critical caveat that any recommendations forthcoming were to be put immediately to the legislature for approval. Thus the Amulree Royal Commission was born. [9]

This imposition was described by the inimitable editorialists at the *Advocate* as constituting the "terms of surrender" for a country desperately in need of outside support. The paper was particularly critical of Alderdice's decision to appoint William Stavert, a Canadian banker, as Newfoundland's representative. [10] This choice may have been Alderdice's way of protecting the process from partisan manipulation, or it might have signalled his anticipation of worst case scenarios from which he wanted some distance. Whatever the motivation, it effectively foreclosed any prospect of a locally directed veto against potentially unpopular final decisions.

Though surrender was indeed in progress, the political game was not over. Through the Amulree Royal Commission the country had one last opportunity to express its collective will, however tentative and uncertain this might be. The records of this inquiry clearly show that whatever the divisions of opinion in the country in the spring and summer of 1933, there was ample opportunity for the people of Newfoundland, at least those equipped to do so—and even some not so well-equipped—to make their case before the Royal Commission and have their concerns met with a large degree of dispassionate neutrality.

The members of the Royal Commission—Lord Amulree, Charles Magrath and Stavert, along with their secretary Peter Clutterbuck—arrived in St. John's early on March 16th. Two weeks later, a public debate was held in St. John's which, judging from the line of questioning the Commissioners pursued with several of the first witnesses, provided a key point of departure for their deliberations. Sponsored jointly by the Llewellyn Club and the Methodist College Literary Institute, this debate considered the proposition that "Newfoundland should be governed by a Commission for a period of ten years." Wide coverage in all three major papers reported the audience was in favour of commission government by a four to one majority. [11] The *Daily News* had promoted the event in advance as addressing a subject "widely discussed at various times in the country's history" and which was now receiving increased attention. The paper suggested its own version of the issue as an "idea of an appointed commission" which it said had "many proponents and a large number of opponents." [12] Such commentary demonstrated that, almost a year after Alderdice's election, the idea was taking on a life of its own. It was now much more present in the public domain and accordingly subject to all sorts of variation and interpretation. As economic and social conditions affecting the population continued to deteriorate, the search for solutions to the country's desperate situation intensified.

That a "large" St. John's audience would give such a strong endorsement of the idea was not lost on either the *Advocate* or the members of the Amulree Commission. The discussion was not only moving forward, but changing along the way. A previous debate on the same question held a month earlier attracted much less attention, and delivered a negative verdict by a much smaller margin. [13] A range of issues was considered at both events. The first debate assumed an appointed commission, in the second the resolution suggested five commissioners, "four of them local and one appointed by the British government." In the first debate, the affirmative side gave voice to many of the themes Coaker had been articulating, and emphasized a view which became something of a refrain during the Amulree hearings, that a government by commission would be desireable because the country was over-governed, "the trappings of an elephant on the back of a cat." [14] In the second debate, the arguments of the winning team focused on the "complete destruction of the morale of the people," which was described as a "vicious outcome of constitutional government." There is no doubt that this public airing of the question put it squarely on the agenda, particularly in St. John's, in a way not previously seen. However, the lines were anything but clear and the direction for the future would remain open for much further reflection, both in public and during the *in camera* sessions before the Royal Commission. The unsettled, and unsettling, nature of the question was reflected in responses to the second debate. Albert Perlin, at the beginning of a career that would see him become Newfoundland's foremost political journalist, wrote a thoughtful and influential

daily column in the *Telegram*, under the byline "Observer."
Perlin declared his strong opposition to the proposal for
commission government and suggested the debate had
been won merely on clever rhetorical tactics. [15] Raymond
Gushue, the young president of the Board of Trade and a
future president of Memorial University, was one of two
speakers in the debate for the negative. He appears to have
partly confirmed Perlin's view in his interview with the
Commission the day after the debate, when he indicated
that his participation on the side against commission government was "not according to my own desires." [16]

It was not likely a coincidence that this public forum
was scheduled during the first days of the Amulree hearings. By the time Raymond Gushue appeared, the
Commissioners had already heard pronouncements from
some of the most prominent people in the country about
suspending responsible government in favour of some sort
of commission scheme. These first witnesses set much of
the tone for the ensuing proceedings, though most who
appeared were not making submissions or being questioned on constitutional matters. The ostensible focus of
Amulree's mandate was, after all, the country's "financial
situation and prospects therein." Questions about changes
to the political system often represented only a brief inter-
lude among other topics. Many of the typed transcripts of
these interviews run twenty to thirty pages in length, and
offer facinating exchanges on a wide range of issues, often
revealing a painful reflection of the country's wounded
body politic. [17]

A STIFF HANDLING

THE COUNTRY'S LAST two conservative Prime Ministers, the north Ireland cousins Alderdice and Monroe, were among the first proponents to advocate a commission form of government in the hearings. According to notes recorded by the Commission secretary, Alderdice declared that as a result of "maladministration of recent years, the people had lost all sense of self-reliance." He reported that the government had embarked on a program to educate the people out of this state, but that in order to make sure there was no political change in the meantime, "there was a good deal to be said for the suggestion that a 'system of government by Commission' should be substituted for the existing form of government until such time as the country had recovered its prosperity." The secretary noted Alderdice was of the view that the country's existing constitution was "satisfactory" provided the government of the day was honest, but that with a dishonest administration, the constitution "left much to be desired." In suggesting the option of government by commission, Alderdice emphasized that such a body should be comprised of Newfoundlanders. [18]

Walter Monroe attributed all of Newfoundland's problems to responsible government. While he felt an election and a referendum should be held on any proposal for commission government, he differed with Alderdice and said such a commission should be led by three or four men appointed from outside the country. Monroe said he was convinced the people would not tolerate reversion to a Crown Colony and would prefer a commission government, even though this would effectively impose colonial status. He had an open mind toward confederation, but in view of the distance from the centre of Canada, and the experience of Nova Scotia in failing to achieve any benefits for itself, Monroe felt on the whole this option was not worthwhile. He emphasized that it was "absolutely impossible" for the country to continue to meet the rate of interest on its debt and insisted that some form of debt conversion or default was necessary. [19]

It is clear from the record of these early sessions that the Commissioners were taken by surprise by the depth of feeling against the existing political system, and were immediately challenged to make sense of an openly-expressed desire for a fundamental overhaul of the machinery of government. In their discussion with A. A. Werlich, manager of the Bank of Montreal, the Commissioners began their efforts to probe for these views. They took turns prompting Werlich for an opinion on the commission government idea and other alternative constitutional options. Werlich said a commission for ten years was a good idea, and he believed it was being supported "even by men who should be in a position to know." Twice asked what the fishermen thought of such an idea, he said it was "too difficult to say" and that he really did not know. When asked by Magrath, the Canadian representative, what reaction there would be to such a proposal, he simply said, "The politicians say we are not competent to govern ourselves." Stavert, Newfoundland's appointee, displayed a certain pre-disposition when he concurred, saying "results have shown that." Amulree then wondered rhetorically if it could be said the people had lost the art of government over time, or whether it was just a recent "spasm of recklessness." [20]

Peter Cashin was another early witness who provided an opportunity for the Commission to explore political questions. Although there is no verbatim account of his testimony, the Commission secretary reported in a detailed note that Cashin emphasized the existing system was too large and expensive for such a small community. He felt the House of Assembly should be reduced to twelve members and the cabinet to six, but suggested that "if it was recognized, as he himself was inclined to recognize, that Newfoundland was not fit to govern itself, then a form of commission government for ten years might be a salvation." Cashin added there was no doubt that such a measure would be greatly resented. Given his future role as a critic of the commission government and a leader of the anti-confederate forces in the late forties, Cashin's testimony here is especially interesting. He went on to say about Canada that the more he visited the place, the more he liked it. According to the secretary's notes:

> He felt that if this country was in the Canadian confederation at the present time, it would be able to carry on successfully. There was no doubt that there was a strong spirit of independence in Newfoundland and the idea of confederation would be bound to cause a certain amount of resentment, but after all, the country had a population of only 250,000 and it was difficult to see how it could emerge by itself from the trouble it had got into.

Cashin said he could not speak with authority on the issue of reverting to a Crown Colony, but if given the choice, he would prefer confederation to such a form of government. [21]

The range of opinion broadened during an interview with J. E. Taylor, from the Canadian Bank of Commerce. Asked if he thought the system of administration was too expensive for a small country, he said yes, adding that it was too "elaborate." Asked what new form of government he would suggest, Taylor answered that the representation should be reduced in the number of districts but the form of representation should stay the same "as today," and financial controls should be strengthened. As the Commissioners were discovering, even among the country's elite, there was no unanimous view of a political remedy for the country's problems. However, there did seem to be agreement that the country should find a way to reduce its interest payments, as Taylor engaged a lengthy discussion on the merits of limited default. He rejected the suggestion that Newfoundland's circumstances could be compared to those in Mexico, a country suffering from continuous political instability. He was not concerned about the credit of Newfoundland, saying it would be "a good thing" if the credit was affected so as to minimize opportunities for further borrowing, and in any case, the merchants could "stand on their own two feet." He also took a liberal view of the spending on relief, saying that the extremity of the conditions facing many people had made such heavy expenditure "absolutely necessary." [22]

Bennett Stafford, manager of the Newfoundland Hotel, where the Commissioners were staying, at first resisted their political inquiries. Asked his view of the general situation, he replied that he had no opinion: "That is what you people are here for, to tell us what we are going to do." When it was suggested the debt was a problem Stafford replied, "We have had a lot of dishonest people here, crooked, doing dishonest things, graft and so on." After suggesting that conversion to lower interest rates would be preferable to default, he volunteered that perhaps a different form of government would safeguard the country's interests. He was asked if this would be permanent. Yes, he said, "for ten years at least, and have no more politicians interfering with our country. I'd like to see someone like yourselves, no favouritism and putting wrong people into jobs." And after that? "Give you another ten, we want some outsiders, good honest men." What about confederation? "It's a debatable question. Newfoundland people are funny, the moment you speak about confederation, they go cracked." Did he mean, then, to do away with the House of Assembly? Certainly.

> Every four years they go to the country and have a political fight and religion enters into it very largely, and a nasty feeling is aroused which doesn't die down for two years. After an election, people would not come into your store because they said you took sides. There is no doubt about it, commission government is the best thing.

Stafford didn't know how many people were in favour of this idea, but said that William Coaker had it "in his mind" and if it was put to a plebiscite to have a commission government for ten years, "you'd win." And what about colonial status? Ninety five per cent of the people, he said, didn't know the difference between a dominion and a colony. [23]

Leonard Outerbridge, owner of one of the country's largest firms, Harvey and Company, was one of many witnesses who sent a written submission and was granted an interview. Later he appeared a second time with a group of merchants and advocated the disenfranchisement of "paupers," but during this first session, Outerbridge focused on his own business activities. He wanted the Commission to understand the problems merchants were having in receiving adequate protection from the police in the face of labour problems. He related an interesting story involving the Longshoreman's union, describing a conflict of interest that arose from his position as chair of the businessmen's committee of the waterfront—the Hauliers Committee—and his duties as chair of the city's Charity Organization Bureau, responsible for distribution of relief. When the Hauliers Committee devised a plan early in 1932 to reduce wages, they expected a strike. Outerbridge wrote to the Inspector General of police asking if they could receive protection for their plan to break the strike by discharging steamers on their own. At the same time, as the head of relief distribution, he wrote to Squires for advice on whether to provide dole to any striking longshoremen. The union somehow received copies of both letters and wrote to the government and the police, threatening that there could be no protection for the merchants in the event of a strike. As a result, Outerbridge complained, the merchants were forced to "cave in" and abandoned their plan to reduce wages.

In his view, "That was really the origin of the riots you may have heard about." He blamed the violence at the Colonial Building on the shortage of police constables and the weak character of the chief of police, who he said was not brave enough and lacked the military training "to dispatch one hundred and fifty policemen and make it look like a thousand." He discussed other issues, including the debt problem, and suggested that any form of default would not harm the bigger merchants, but the smaller ones like his brother, who were operating on consignment, could be put out of business if their advances were called in. He also complained that it was impossible to get the right type of men into politics because "the efficent man is very busy," and the political scene was not an inviting one: "I suppose for example, what I have said here—it is very reasonable—if I said that outside here, I might as well pack up and get out." [24]

Eric Bowring, a prominent businessman who had organized meetings in opposition to Squires in 1931, spoke very plainly in his view of the problems associated with the political system. "The average person here is such that we ought never to have had self-government, we are not fit for self-government." To illustrate the point, he told a story of the time he went hunting along the southern shore from St. John's and had to drive about twenty miles with a warden from the area who acted as his guide. During conversation, he asked how the people felt about the government. The warden replied, "We are going to throw the government out, they are no good. The government bull is here and there has not been a calf from here down to Trepassey." Bowring said he was struck by how "perfectly frightful" it was to have to deal with "those fellows." When asked how he would overcome this situation, he said:

> I hope you will go the limit as far as our constitution allows, to put this colony back as a Crown Colony or government by commission, have somebody who cannot be removed by the hopeless will of the people.

The Commissioners wanted to know how such a proposal would be received. Would there be objections? Bowring thought that because of sentimental reasons, "you might get through government by commission," because it would only be temporary and people could see the end of it, "whereas you would never get through a reversion to a Crown Colony." Magrath asked if the situation could be saved with three or four aggressive men in the House of

Assembly. Bowring replied that they would never get elected if they told the truth. [25]

Bowring was followed by the interview with the Board of Trade's Raymond Gushue, who reviewed how the Board operated, and had a lengthy discussion concerning the activites of the fish exporters and the difficulties in getting them to act together to set common standards for the industry. Eventually the talk turned to politics and he said that he had participated in the public debate on commission government, leading the side against the proposition, although this did not reflect his real view, as "I did not want to be in on it." He said he thought the feeling in the country was that "nothing can be done under our present system." The Commissioners wanted to know if such a proposal would pass in the House of Assembly and whether there would be general support for it from the people. Gushue replied that it could be passed by a government and would not need to go before the country in a plebiscite because "you could not expect any intelligent response from the electorate." He believed this might only be a temporary solution though. Ultimately, the country would at some time become part of Canada.

Just when it may have seemed to the Commissioners they were uncovering a certain degree of common opinion, their line of questioning was challenged. R. F. Horwood, a St. John's businessman who owned a sawmill in Notre Dame Bay, was not prepared to concede the logic of radical proposals, at least not initially. Following a detailed review of the timber industry and the debt problem, in which Horwood argued for reducing the interest rate by following Britain's lead in engineering conversion loans on its war debt, the discussion turned to the political system. Horwood had submitted a letter in which he criticized the politicians. The Commissioners wanted to know whether, with two Houses of parliament and all the related expenses, he had considered if such a large administration was necessary. He answered that he failed to see how it was possible to have democratic government without sufficient representation. He said the challenge was to make a constitution that would "protect the country from itself and its pirates" and that would secure continuation of responsible government. He was asked if this was an alternative to a commission form of government, and replied that there could not be a government without the consent of the people.

> You will have troubles for the future if you do. You know the history of these forms of government. You have them in Africa and India and you know that the struggle has been to get out of the grip of the conditions that have been brought about, and it would be a struggle here for years.

The Commissioners were not entirely dissuaded, and asked if there might be an advantage to a ten year period of relief from politics. Horwood then relented on the larger point and ventured that if political life was going to be killed off, it would likely take fifty years and not ten. He admitted a certain bitterness in this view that he attributed to his experience as a defeated candidate. Finally, he referred to the effects of the Hollis Walker report. "He scattered the results all over the island but no action was taken when iniquities were being perpetrated all over the country." The result, he suggested, "depraved the public mind." [26]

It was not uncommon for contradictory opinions to be expressed by a witness. Marmaduke Winter, a businessman and member of the Upper House, talked in circles when the discussion got around to politics. He indicated he had attended the public debate on commission government and then defensively stated he was not a politician, as politics had been reserved mostly for "a few lawyers." He felt that the more control of the country was taken out of the hands of local people the better. But when asked how the people felt about either confederation or the commission idea, he said there would not be support for confederation and that he agreed with the view that "we should have our own government," even though people were "sick of the politicians." [27]

J. S. Ayre, another powerful merchant and a member of Alderdice's cabinet, followed Winter. Ayre was forthright in the view, "gaining ground more and more," that a commission form of government was desirable. He was asked for details and suggested it be comprised of three men. Outsiders? "Yes, definitely." Businessmen? "Why not?" It was put to him by Magrath that in the spirit of democracy, it would be difficult to have outsiders brought in and public men agree to be ruled by them. Ayre's view of that was simple and by now familiar, at least from certain quarters: "We're not fit to govern ourselves…what we want is very stiff handling." He didn't withhold blame for this situation from his own kind. He said that the system was corrupted by the paying of private commissions and that it would have to be admitted that whenever a corporation wanted a bill passed, "grasping politicians will do anything." He said he shared the general demoralization of the people.

> I have been acquainted personally with many members who have composed the various governments that have got into power for a number of years, but even knowing

them, I still contend there are a lot of them, too many
of them, who are simply out to do the country. [28]

Although at this point the hearings were still in an
early stage, certain unmmistakeable themes were beginning to emerge, albeit from a limited pool of merchant-
elite witnesses. But many of these recurring issues would
echo and be reinforced as the Commission made its way
across the island and returned for a second round of hearings later in St. John's. During the rest of the sessions and
in the correspondence received, the Commission heard
from wider sections of the population. Unfortunately,
when visiting the outports and speaking with fishermen,
the Commissioners did not pursue the questions on which
they had seemed anxious to get a reading from the St.
John's elite. [29]

TEN HONEST MEN

TWENTY FISHERMEN WERE interviewed in small groups in
four communities: Carbonear, Heart's Content, Bonavista
and Catalina. With the exception of a brief exchange concerning Coaker, not once, during many long hours of discussion, was a question raised about political or constitutional matters. The testimonies of the fishermen did, however, catalogue a systematic critique of the structure of the
fishery and the exploitation they suffered at the hands of
the merchants and exporters. There were continuous complaints about the cost of living, the cost of gear and supplies and the practices of profiteering middlemen, and
numerous appeals for independent inspectors and supervision of culling methods. The exchanges were replete with
self-conscious expressions of pride and anger at the
absence of justice, along with demands for minimal

standards of fair treatment. Much of this evidence found its way directly into the Amulree report and provided the basis for its most enlightened analysis and informed recommendations. The only oblique reference to the lack of representation of fishermen's concerns in the political system occurred in Carbonear when two fishermen, George Parsons and Herb Davies, were asked whether there was not at one time a union to protect their interests. The reply was that "Sir William Coaker went into politics." And before that? "He was a great help to the fishermen…if Sir William had continued, it would have been of great benefit to the fishermen of this country." [30]

The Commissioners did, however, engage in political discussions with non-elite sectors of the population when they interviewed representatives from the most important union organizations in the country. [31] These sessions captured a tremendous variety of opinion, with views addressing the full range of political options. But there was also a reluctance to be drawn into openly political questions, in clear contrast to a more primary concern with bread and butter issues. Michael Coady, for instance, of the Longshoremen's union in St. John's, was asked if his union had formed an opinion on the difficulties facing the country. He said no. He was then asked what he thought personally and said he could not say, he "could not deal with anything like that." When he was asked what his men were saying or whether they were saying anything, he replied: "Some of our men do and some will not. We do not believe in cutting men's wages." For this union leader, the only political issue that mattered was getting paid a fair wage. [32]

James Power of the Coopers' union in St. John's said he had no political opinions of his own, but when asked about confederation, volunteered that it should not be left to ordinary people.

There should be a body of intelligent men to consider that. They know what is good for the country, not the ordinary man, they do not know. There should be somebody like that, intelligent men, outstanding men who will take the matter and discuss it and see what it would mean to this country. You could then put it to a vote when the people understood it. [33]

Not all the union representatives interviewed were so reticent in expressing political opinions. In Grand Falls a delegation of five men representing three unions from the paper mill was divided. Cater, from the Papermakers, first ventured that the people were overtaxed because "our system of government as we have known it for the last twenty five years is a washout." He was asked in what way was the government a washout. Perhaps, he said, he should not have put it that way. "There is something wrong. There may not be anything wrong with the form of government, but there is something wrong with the way it is carried out." The group was asked whether they all shared this opinion. Scott, from the Amalgamated Trades, said yes. However Wall, from the same union, had a different view and put a fine point on the matter:

> The trouble with Newfoundland is that she has got the trappings of an elephant on the back of a cat...what Newfoundland wants is a commission of ten honest men and pay them. [34]

The Commission travelled on to Buchans, and then to Corner Brook. There, George Smith, a worker representative from the paper mill, responded to the Commissioners' questions directly. His group of three was asked if they gave any attention to the general situation of the country. He replied naturally they thought about it. And did they come to any conclusions? He said, personally, he did not see any objection to the present form of government, "providing the right men could be found to represent the country," which seemed to him to be the main difficulty. He was asked what complaint he had against the "class of men" who were being elected. "I imagine they have too many outside interests. To my mind a man who represents people should be a person who is not tied up with outside interests. He should be free lance." Did he and his friends take any steps to make their opinions felt? "No, I cannot say that we have. We are very tolerable in Newfoundland." Most of the discussion with this group involved issues of working conditions and wage scales. The union had been on strike the previous year and were now fighting a proposed thirty per cent pay cut. Smith had just returned from St. John's where he had lobbied the government to have the eight-hour day "standardized and included in the constitution." [34]

It is clear from these transcripts and in the manner of their inquiries that the members of the Royal Commission were on a bit of a fishing expedition. At times they coaxed witnesses with gently placed suggestions. In some sessions the record shows they were very persistent in following a particular line of questioning. Aside from general information gathering, the political direction was toward a definition of how far constitutional change could be pushed, and specifically, what were the features and parameters of this idea of commission government? To what extent was it a viable alternative? Was it, perhaps, the only alternative? And what did the witnesses think other people were thinking? Was a referendum necessary? How would the membership of a commission government be decided? A veritable Pandora's box of constitutional options lay on the table.

And the untested and nebulously defined idea of commission was a tantalizing point of entry.

In their struggle to achieve clarity the Commissioners may even have converted some to the commission idea. It may be generous to suggest this would have been a case of unintended consequences, but it is based on two assumptions from reading the transcripts. The first, and this is corroborated by diplomatic records discussed below, is that the Commissioners were not, at least at this time, conducting their inquiry with any kind of hidden agenda. [36] Secondly, they were genuinely challenged by both the despondent mood of the people and the conceptual, philosophical and practical problems associated with an ill-defined proposal for constitutional change. It would have been impossible for them not to attempt to come to terms with the fact that the idea of commission government was capturing people's imaginations, however unattractive its undemocratic nature might appear.

On certain occasions, the Commissioners' approach was a leading one. It is sometimes difficult to divine their purpose from the transcripts, but it is apparent they were pushing for an honest expression of views on issues not always freely addressed in public debate. In an exchange with one of only three women interviewed in the hearings, Mrs. J. G. Muir, the Relief Commissioner for St. John's and secretary of the Charity Organization Bureau, the Commissioners received an inside glimpse on the workings of the city's overburdened relief system. [37] Mrs. Muir reported that conditions in the city were "worse than ever" and described the difficulties in administering a program of food rations through local grocers at a value of $1.60 per person per month to, in her most recent count, 1,592 families, or about 5,000 people. [38] She suggested a big part of the problem was people coming from the outports looking for work and finding none, and having to live overcrowded in "shacks" that were "not fit for human beings." The Commission secretary, Clutterbuck, picked up on a reference she made to an increase in rates that had been made the previous year as a result of the politicians having to "give way on political grounds." He asked if the people who received relief should be deprived of the right of voting at elections. Mrs. Muir replied she did not know. "I really do not see why they should have a vote at all, they are of no assistance to the country at all. They are the crowd who are really always looking for dole."

Amulree then followed up by asking Mrs. Muir if such a restriction might be applied only in a given voting year. She said "In some cases, yes, but in others, no." He suggested that any such rule would have to be applied to all equally. She agreed this might be a problem. "Yes, it would be too bad to deprive some of them of their vote when they have been genuinely forced to seek relief." The chairman then reviewed the practice in England of the "old election roll call," whereby persons on relief in an election year were disqualified from voting, and suggested that discretion would have to be exercised by authorities in any such scheme. Mrs. Muir agreed, "because I think there are families getting relief through no fault of their own, and on the other hand, others make you believe they will never be any better." It is not likely the British interlocuters had it seriously in mind that singling out the poor for penalty by removing their franchise was a viable option. Even though some of their witnesses were precisely of this view, [39] such probing would have given them another window on the greater issue of whether everyone in the country should lose their vote, this being the premise of all the talk about government by commission.

One important example of the Commissioners' occasionally zealous technique is apparent in a long session with Charles Jeffrey, the editor of the *Evening Telegram*. Jeffrey was interviewed during the second round in St. John's in June, after the Commission's trip to Halifax and Ottawa, where they continued their fact-finding and sought the views of the Canadian government on the possible sale of Labrador and terms that might be negotiated on confederation. Jeffrey was virtually browbeaten into giving up his efforts to argue for confederation and conceding instead that commission government was a more realistic option. The Commissioners had not only found the Canadian government unwilling to offer any further assistance, either with the raising of new loans or opening up longer term discussions, they had also come to the conclusion that confederation was a non-starter among Newfoundlanders. In an uncharacteristic outburst during a rambling discussion about the merits of democracy, Amulree suggested that there could be no "real check on good government" and demanded to know from Jeffrey whether that was "the reason why some people have been writing to the press and speaking out at public meetings in favour of commission government. Is that not right?" Sounding very much defeated, the editor replied, "Yes quite. I feel it would do us no harm, if for a period it were possible to suspend the present form of government and to have this country placed under a commission." As an afterthought, Jeffrey insisted that such an action could never be carried out without taking the opinion of the people. In an interesting footnote to this exchange, Stavert responded to Jeffrey's suggestion that Canadian politicians

were no more honest than those in Newfoundland by saying, "Let us leave honesty out and say more experienced." [40]

KEEP US FROM A SHIPWRECK

WHILE THE COMMISSIONERS carried on their busy schedule of meetings there was also a massive amount of docu-
mentation to be reviewed. Detailed memoranda were prepared from every government department, many of which
were followed up by interviews with senior civil servants
and such technical experts as were available. They also
received in the course of their stay a total of forty-nine letters from individuals and groups covering a vast range of
material, with suggestions from everything to the harbour
pilot operation at St. John's to the co-operative movement, agricultural development, and proposals for the
manufacture of fish meal. Many of these submissions
decried various ills, including the denominational control
of education, patronage in the civil service, a decay of
morals associated with the dole, the high rate of customs
tariffs, and even one complaint from a group of St. John's
businessmen concerning the devaluation of the Canadian
dollar and its negative effects on the purchasing power of
Newfoundlanders, who had not been consulted on
Canadian monetary policy. [41]

Of these submissions, seven contained direct suggestions for a commission form of government, three were in
favour of confederation and two suggested that there could
be no real alternative to the existing political system.
Scathing indictments of political practices were common.
And numerous submissions from the outports contained
evidence of oppressive behaviour by merchants. The
Harbour Grace branch of the Co-operative Self-Help
Association sent in a resolution adopted at a "largely

attended" public meeting. The "be-it-resolved" clauses outlined those factors which were not the source of the country's "deplorable financial and economic position," including the wealth of natural resources, the willingness of the people to apply to any form of work or labour, and a general "sympathy for the lot of producers in their unequal struggle." The motion went on to identify the primary cause of the present condition as "extreme selfishness of these, our leading people, politicians and unscrupulous businesmen who have been tacitly entrusted with the management and direction of our economic processes." It concluded with a call for action:

> The time has come when the full force of the laws of the land should be brought to bear upon the well-being of the whole people and not only of a select few people and interests.

The Victoria Lodge of the Society of United Fishermen sent in a similar appeal and directed its frustration at the pleasant words of welcome that Alderdice had reportedly offered the Commission.

> In your opening speech you stated that the Prime Minister said the people were meeting the situation with a determination to overcome the difficulty and bearing their burdens as cheerfully as possible. Maybe he is, but the people are not very cheerful around here. They don't know what to do or which way to turn.

The letter went on to ask if there was a law against profiteering and suggested, in view of the prices being paid fishermen, that it would be "a move in the right direction to put it in force." The Commissioners were told to call up fishermen for interviews on the "full particulars" of the industry and were reminded in closing, "We wish to impress upon you that the cheerfulness Mr. Alderdice referred to is just about expired."

Alderdice's personal business activity was the subject of a note prepared by the Commission secretary who reported a visit by Robert Thorne and George Eustace of Torbay. These men wanted to bring to the Commissioners' attention a number of matters concerning the unfair organization of the fishery. In addition to complaints about poor grading and classification, the absence of foreign buyers to provide competition for local exporters, and unfair price levels that reduced men to "starving" while merchants reported sizeable profits, the men had a specific grievance with the Prime Minister. They said that Alderdice's Cordage Company had a monopoly on the sale of rope, nets, twine and related supplies in their area and that this company would only sell these goods wholesale instead of directly to fishermen. According to the secretary's note, given the dire distress of the fishermen, it was in their view a "great shame allowing for a rake-off for middlemen, and it would certainly help the fishermen if arrangements could be made to get material direct from the Cordage Company."

The concerns of fishermen were addressed by numerous correspondents, and these were often tied directly to the fate of the country. Albert Moulton, who had been fishing for forty-nine years in Burin, wrote to suggest that the Board of Trade should "give themselves and the fishermen a thorough consideration" in the interest of ensuring that "justice is meted out to all." He believed the only issue that mattered was not how much money could be made in the fishery, "but rather, how can we save our country and our people." A Mr. Oke in Fogo wrote to complain that the exporters in his district were harder on the fishermen than they need be, "and if they would only give us a bit of British fair play, we would work together for the good of all." He appealed to the Commissioners to give the fishermen "a thought in your work" and to advise ways and means "so that we may provide for our families and keep England's oldest colony from being a shipwreck."

Many of the letters, both from businessmen and others, emphasized the critical importance of reducing the interest rate on the debt as a means of allowing the country to remain solvent. George Ball of Codroy, who described himself as a "keen patriot" with experience in the fishery for seventy years, and whose only son was resting in the soil as a result of the war, warned against doing nothing to reduce the debt burden. He wrote that a compromise had to be reached, otherwise the country's "last cent must be drawn from the poor man and his family to enrich the already rich bondholders." In case the issue was not clear enough, he added:

> I need not point out to learned men of your type that the burden we are bearing is closely akin to tyranny and history tells us in no uncertain terms what such will lead to. CF France and the revolution; CF Russia and Czarism and taxation; CF Spain and its reaction.

On the subject of history, the Commission received a letter from Robert Job, a director of one of Newfoundland's oldest family fishing firms, who wrote that he agreed with his own great grandfather, William Carson, who a century earlier had agitated for representative, but not full responsible government. He complained that the existing "wide franchise, which includes even illiteral voting entirely free from any educational standard, seems to have hardly justified itself." He then suggested that for a period of "say five or ten years" the present form of government be suspended and the administration of the state's affairs be vested in a "businesslike Commission" composed partly of trained appointees from Britain and partly of local appointees, "with a preponderance of the former." Thomas White, of St. George's, wrote in to suggest the importance of cultivating local foods and the need for establishing a flour mill. As for the best "form of government," he suggested a commission having "dictatorial power" and the "welfare of Newfoundland at heart." He cautiously admitted that with such an arrangement, he feared a "German general in the French war camp type."

Amid all the earnest messages from the public and the mass of barren bureaucratic papers, there are portions of the correspondence to the Commissioners that must have made for compelling reading. Alive with literary allusions and often displaying a language of natural poetry, these pages would have held their own alongside the intensity of any of the *in camera* sessions. George Dawe, who signed as "a fishmonger" from Corner Brook, told a sad tale of having invested and lost his life savings in attempts to develop methods for processing fresh instead of salted fish. But he was undaunted and believed still that this was the way of the future. He enlisted Tennyson in his appeal for new approaches to the country's oldest industry: "The old order changeth, yielding place to new, / And God fulfills himself in many ways, / Lest one good custom should corrupt the world." Hardly Job's illiterates.

Arthur English, from Doyle's Station, wrote a memo on the importance of land cultivation and of introducing new farming methods. He summarized by invoking Catherine of Russia, whom he quoted writing to Potemkin:

"Courage, with courage, all can be repaired, even a disaster." And so it was with Newfoundland: "So can Newfoundland repair her damages, but to courage must be added intelligence, or we may be knocking our heads off against a wall." One other example of very nearly inspired prose is found in a long letter from Max Small of Moreton's Harbour (see Appendix B). This submission draws a righteous historical account of the nefarious deeds of the "powers that be" and the evidently well-deserved "contempt" held for them by the people. A furious rage directed equally toward the behaviour of Coaker, Squires and the merchants, the letter stands as an exhibit in the people's case against their own government.

AN IRISH WAY OF ANSWERING

IT IS NOT really possible to do justice to the literally thousands of pages of testimony and documents prepared and presented to the Royal Commission. Any survey is by definition selective and fragmentary. But from even a brief sample it is obvious that the presence of the Commission had generated a tremendous amount of interest and a great deal of anxiety as to its findings. Everyone knew the stakes were extremely high, and there would have been a lot of guessing and rumours about the intentions of the Commissioners, particularly by those who had spent any time in their presence. Whatever was thought of their methods or inclination, there seemed to be a general deference to the wisdom and impartiality of this small group of outsiders, sent by the benevolent hand of the Mother country to arbitrate what would have to be a binding solution. The country was clearly prepared, no matter where this would lead, to take its cue as to what should happen next from the Royal Commission.

Two final interviews are worthy of note in this context. These are instructive in reading the transcripts of the Commission's hearings as the vehicle which set up the findings and recommendations of the Amulree report. Both offer a reference for assessing an important memorandum that was prepared by the secretary, Peter Clutterbuck, for the Commissioners during their final meeting in St. John's in September. (See Appendix D.) This memo summarized the evidence presented on the options for changing the country's constitution and outlined the various legal and technical alternatives before the Commission in considering any such change. Its existence provides key material evidence on the thinking behind the Commission's deliberations.

Albert Perlin was one of those who sent a letter outlining a number of suggestions for addressing the country's grave situation. These were themes that he was regularly stressing in his daily column in the *Telegram*. They included a range of measures that he felt would work toward rehabilitation, without having to take any drastic action on the country's constitution. He suggested the appointment of a small body of experts that would prepare a written constitution containing severe penalties for "graft" and eliminating the practice of local politicians distributing government funds; a progressive system of education to improve the "attitude" of the people; and the use of broadcast educational programmes to inform people about the country's serious problems. In a summary review of his proposals, one of the Commissioners said he had suggested commission government. He objected and said he did not. [42] At this stage, as he had been stating in his columns, he had not been dissuaded from his resistance toward the commission idea, and was not about to change his view during the course of his hearing. His influential voice of principled opposition was one of only a few in what must have seemed like a growing cacophony for radical action. When later in the summer he did come round to the proposition in his column, as a result of reported developments related to British intentions, his changed view would have been all the more significant in building a perceived basis of support for the Commission's recommendations.

Harris Mosdell was the only independent Member of the House in 1933. His interview with the Commissioners toward the end of their hearings must have given them pause for thought. He told them Newfoundland's problems were caused by an absolute lack of organization combined with being a country "on the fringe of BNA Confederacy trying to duplicate the whole panoply of government." In his view, confederation was the only viable option. It would pass in a vote outside St. John's, and as a result carry the country. When he was asked whether he had any other alternatives in mind, he replied, "What other alternative can there be, if you'll pardon my Irish way of answering. This Commission cannot say we've looked you over and find you're unfit for self-government." The Commissioners tried to play to his obvious disdain for the commission idea by suggesting that any amendment to the Letters Patent would probably be strongly resisted. He said he did not know that it would, but his own reaction to the suggestion was hostile "because you are maintaining the old order, not doing anything in the way of radical change." He believed once a commission had re-organized the country, it would just be handed back to the same "insular bunch." But Mosdell's views were perhaps most challenging when he concluded his interview by putting his own opinions in the background and spoke directly to the Commissioners about their work and the process ahead of them:

> We are rather shocked at our position. Tremendous importance is attached to the work you gentlemen are doing and the anticipation of the report you are expected to make, and I do not think you will find anybody standing out against the adoption of the report so long as it is reasonable. It would be a great mistake in my opinion...to delay any material part of the programme. That is necessary for the rehabilitation of Newfoundland, whether it is to take the line of confederation and direct action of the legislature, or as the result of a plebiscite, or whether a commission form of government. Whatever is in your minds a definite plan should be adopted, the country should be told it, and the country should be urged and recommended to adopt it immediately. We are frightful people in Newfoundland for looking forward to the future and hoping the best is going to turn up without doing a great deal to realize our hopes. [43]

In this, Mosdell was giving the Commission its marching orders. His remarks also addressed the key points of complexity in the situation, which were in turn reflected in the substance of the memorandum prepared for the Commissioners later in the fall. First, despite the posturing confidence of many of the leading merchants, there were very real and significant long term problems with implementing the commission idea. Secondly, nobody was certain, not even those with definite opinions, what the best solution would be to address the political issues that virtually everyone identified as part of the larger problem. Mosdell, like Perlin, represented a substantial voice of opposition to government by commission, but he too would not stand fast in this resistance. Third, and this was a palpable feeling that is evoked in the pages of the testimony, the population was depending on Amulree for a decisive result that would provide direction and clarity. Finally, the Commission should not dither. Whatever the mechanism for implementing its programme, it had to be initiated immediately.

The September memorandum, despite its bureaucratic jargon and mind-set, is remarkable in the extent to which these elements were combined in a coherent presentation of the options facing the Commissioners. Perhaps more remarkable, is that its author, Clutterbuck, came down on the side of a minimalist definition of what shape a commission should take. His conclusion clearly suggests that in order to prevent a violent reaction, and as a means of causing the least embarrassment to both Britain and Newfoundland, it would be necessary and desireable to avoid the suppression of the legislature. Although there is no record of a submission that was apparently made by Coaker to the Commission, it is likely that it was his often-stated appeal to maintain some semblance of democratic process, combined with a warning about the consequences of not doing so, which resulted in the emphasis in the memo on anticipating the danger of partisan "stampeding." [44] The memo left open the question of whether a referendum would be necessary. As it turned out, the Amulree Commission rejected the advice of its secretary, and instead followed the instructions given to it by the British treasury through the Chancellor of the Exchequer. In so doing it was bound to accept Mosdell's admonitions to act with haste and to get the job done.

None to Shed a Tear

THE AMULREE HEARINGS concluded on June 23rd, 1933. The country then waited for five months in anxious anticipation for the report, published and released in London, Ottawa and St. John's on November 21st. In the interim, debate continued in the pages of the press, with the *Advocate* carrying the commission banner and insisting that no action be taken without the consent of the people, as if it feared a losing battle on this principle. Perlin's columns in the *Telegram* contained a rigourous analysis of the various undertakings likely to be initiated by the Commission, focusing on the conversion of loans, measures for control of the treasury, and until he changed his mind in July a strong rejection of the idea of government by commission. [1] The *Daily News* ran comparative commentaries on fascism, socialism and democracy and the relevance of changing world conditions to Newfoundland's situation, noting that the "political student" would be struck by "the way in which democracy is fading from the earth." The paper observed that the dictatorships of Russia, Italy and Germany were being joined by Britain and the United States, where the people had consented to the "semi-dictatorship of national administrations." These developments, it suggested, bore lessons for Newfoundland, where the question was being asked of whether democracy was doomed to yield to "some form of autocracy"—namely, a government by commission. [2]

All this rather detached discussion was rudely interrupted by a report in the middle of July that J. H. Thomas, the British Secretary of State for the Dominions, and a close Labour colleague of Prime Minister Ramsay MacDonald, had stated in the House of Commons that the Royal Commission would be reporting soon on whether Newfoundland was to remain a Dominion or become a Crown Colony. All three papers jumped on the suggestion that Amulree's mandate included the possibility of reversion to colonial status, ignoring the scope of constitutional change otherwise evident in the options being widely debated. The *Advocate* said that to entertain the idea "would mean confusion worse confounded…a humiliation of the worst type ever administered to a British people" and also, that it was pointless to discuss such a possibility, because it would be "resisted by the united strength of the whole people." The paper insisted that only the commission it had been promoting for so long would be acceptable. However on this occasion it recommended the composition of such a body to be three members and the governor, with the same power and authority as that normally resting with the legislature. Such a model may have represented less of a loss in status than a Crown Colony, but it was beginning to appear nearly indistinguishable. [3]

Perlin in the *Telegram* questioned whether this was another "slip of the tongue" for which the Secretary of State was famous, or if in fact this was within the Commission's terms of reference. For Perlin, such a question of reversion was "too ridiculous" and "definitely out of court." Despite his dismissal of the report—and this was likely the effect of the "slip" desired by British authorities—over the next several days, the columnist admitted he was provoked to re-consider the commission idea as an alternative to Crown Colony status. Perlin then reviewed what he acknowledged as Coaker's proposal.

While insisting he did not believe such a system would be recommended by Amulree, he began articulating the positive aspects of a form of political control that would not abrogate democratic rights but would nevertheless delegate the task of overhauling the country's administrative system to an appointed committee. Perlin eventually arrived at the position, maintained in future columns, that "if it be necessary to limit the responsibility of our people in connection with their government, a commission is unquestionably the best way out." [4] In this process, he was engaged in a kind of catch-up with Coaker, and a pursuit of precisely the issues confronting the Royal Commission.

Shortly thereafter reports appeared from London that the Commission had submitted its report and that its recommendations included the suspension of the constitution, and the handing over of the country's administration to a nominated commission with full powers. The *Advocate* labelled this a "bolt from the blue" and, noting that Stavert categorically denied any part of the report had been completed, called on Alderdice to make a statement on the issue without delay. [5] Perlin greeted the "rumours" as an indication that the country must be prepared for proposals that would place "very definite restrictions on our political independence." [6] This, he was now convinced, would be a good thing. As the country drifted into the fall of 1933, it would appear that something resembling a generally existing consensus on the desired political outcome was in place.

DOCUMENTS BEHIND DOCUMENTS

IN THE MEANTIME, the members of the Commission were preparing for a final visit to St. John's in mid-September, to consult with Alderdice and consolidate their findings.

Diplomatic records clearly show that at the end of August Neville Chamberlain gave Amulree final and definitive instructions from the British government as to what should be contained in the Commission's report. In a telegram to Amulree that historian Peter Neary has described as "the document behind the document," Chamberlain outlined a strategy for a disguised default orchestrated by the British treasury. [7] All outstanding loans would be converted to new bonds issued at a lower rate of interest (the reduction in rates went from a high of six per cent down to three and a quarter, with this later reduced to three). Chamberlain indicated that his office had been preoccupied with the necessity of preventing default by Newfoundland for some time, especially following the failure of the Canadian government to co-operate in providing interim assistance on the debt payments due in July. He felt a unilateral default "would be so damaging to Imperial credit that we ought to take all possible measures to avert its consequences." This conservative view was consistent with his position as the leading Tory in the British administration. He then laid out the political side of the plan, one that would allow the "Mother country" to save face with the bondholders on a "technical default" because "the system of government under which the default had arisen would for the time being have ceased to function."

Chamberlain in fact made it clear that the regular reports from Amulree, including a detailed memo dated July 17th, were the real documents behind the document that would become the Amulree report. He said he was persuaded by Amulree's July memo that Newfoundland had reached a point of insolvency wherein the "existing order of government" could neither meet its debt payments nor provide the "most meagre social services." In addition, Chamberlain had "formed the impression too that it would not be repugnant to the Islanders to be relieved for the time being of responsibilities which are beyond them." Although Amulree's July memo was not explicit on this point, minutes from a meeting of senior British officials where this memo was reviewed, reflected their understanding that "the bulk of the evidence tendered to the Commission had been in favour of 'Commission Government', i.e., a form of government which would place the administration of the country in the hands of five or six men and would give the Island a rest from politics." [8]

The notes from these discussions show that Newfoundlanders themselves gave shape to the solution ultimately constructed and refined by Chamberlain and his bureaucrats. Amulree had reported as early as April, after only a few days of hearings, that "in the opinion of many, the Dominion has become unsuited for responsible government," and that "government by Commission for a term of years" was "much discussed locally." [9] In numerous dispatches through the period of the hearings, Amulree had promoted a variety of schemes that would allow for limited default without impairing Newfoundland's constitutional status. These reports are neutral in tone and consistent with the records and notes kept of the hearings. Amulree's memos can only be read as advancing the case for a commission form of government insofar as the witnesses were advocating it.

Through Chamberlain's private instructions to Amulree, the September meeting of the Commission was given a programme that effectively pre-empted not only the memorandum prepared by Clutterbuck, but also the ability of the Commissioners to independently reach their own conclusion. Significantly, the decision to write a report that would recommend the suspension of the legislature was taken over the objections of the Canadian member, Charles Magrath. The day after their final meeting Magrath wrote a letter to Clutterbuck in which he put on the record objections to commission government he had stated the night before. He said that "control by the elected representatives of the people" was an issue he had fought when he was a member of the legislature in the North West Territories forty years earlier. Despite this dissenting view, Macgrath did not want to take the course of signing the report with "certain stated reservations." He felt there was "far too much involved in this Newfoundland situation" for the Commission to produce anything other than a unanimous recommendation. [10]

Two weeks later, Magrath wrote Amulree to suggest that the draft report be "modified" to lessen its emphasis on the dishonesty of politicians and the "willingness of many to be bribed with public funds." He said there was no point in exposing to the outside world stories of stupidity, graft and other weaknesses. "Frankly, it is a subject in which I am not interested. Every nation seems to go through a certain amount of it before becoming more or less competent." Magrath concluded by reminding the chairman of his belief in confederation as the best solution, but noted that virtually no one in Newfoundland seemed interested in the idea, and commission government was "the desire of nearly all who appeared before the Commission." He thought it best to leave the final preparation of the report to the two representatives whose countries had a direct stake in the matter. [11] In the meantime, Amulree was kept busy negotiating the support of Alderdice for the recommendations as developed by

Chamberlain. These efforts succeeded through a last-minute direct appeal from Prime Minister Ramsay Macdonald and an assurance of a *quid pro quo* that would see Alderdice and two of his ministers appointed to the new regime. The preparations for the publication and delivery of the report continued. [12]

As the diplomatic manoevering and bargaining continued, uncertainty and anxiety on the home front was unabated. The *Advocate* continued to campaign aggressively for commission government, promoting the idea as one which was continuing to gain favour with the population, and citing various examples of such support. It emphasized the necessity of a plebiscite to confirm and validate this widely-held opinion. [13] The *Telegram*'s Perlin staked out different ground. He reported a conversation he had with a member of the House of Assembly who would not support a proposal for commission without a plebiscite. Perlin was adamant that a commission would not be recommended, but argued that if it were, it would reflect that democracy, as evidenced especially by events in Europe, was becoming an anachronism. [14]

In Newfoundland's case, Perlin wrote, governments were only democratic to the extent they were elected, and all subsequent decisions were taken in the name of the people without any need for recourse to further consultation. Consequently, if the existing Parliament voted to undertake extraordinary measures, particularly to alter the country's constitution, it had a right to do so consistent with normal practice. In an emergency, "actions otherwise unconstitutional may, in a period of crisis, be sanctioned by the constitution," which, he pointed out, was not written and therefore "open to numerous constructions and wide liberties." Perlin cited the example of the United States where extraordinary powers to fight the effects of the Depression were being granted to the presidential office of Franklin Roosevelt, with the support of court rulings validating the principle of emergency power. In addition to arguing that a plebiscite would be costly and a waste of time, he warned against "unpatriotic politicians" attempting to persuade the people to vote against their own best interests. He offered a view in direct conflict with that of the *Advocate*:

> In the circumstances, whatever drastic changes may be recommended by the Royal Commission, always provided that they are acceptable to well-informed and patriotic opinion, ought to be made effective by the Legislature without recourse to that doubtful medium of expressing sound opinion, the plebiscite.

Coaker intervened directly for the last time in the public debate before the report was released through a column he wrote responding to requests from numerous people whom he said asked his opinion of the situation facing the country. He addressed the financial crisis at some length and offered a number of suggestions focusing on the fishery and calling for the Royal Commission to recommend reducing the rate of interest on debt charges as a means of avoiding an outright default. Coaker concluded by returning to the political issues facing the country and sounded a clarion call which the Commissioners, and their superiors in London, would have found reassuring in the midst of their own final preparations:

> Party government must be dispensed with for at least ten years and provision made for Government by an elected commission presided over by the Governor. The

country is generally sick and disgusted with Party Government and the present generation would gladly agree to a suspension of both Chambers of the Legislature for the next ten years, if not longer. The greatest curse that could be inflicted on a suffering and agonized people would be to bring about a general election and replace the ins by the outs...The future welfare of this country depends largely upon the recommendations of the Royal Commission. If it is a milk-and-water scribble it will damn the country and sour feelings toward the Home Government and if recommendations are not possible that will be certain of fulfilment and provide means for the rehabilitation of the fisheries, a forty per cent reduction of the interest on the public debt, and a suspension of the animosities, intrigues, patronage and boodle of political office seekers, then all our sufferings will have been in vain and a gloom deeper and blacker than any hitherto experienced will envelop the country and the people. [15]

News was received in early October that it would be some time yet before the report would be released. Accounts in the papers suggest that rumours were rampant as people busied themselves with speculation on who might fill the seats of an expected commission government. The British Trade Commissioner H. F. Gurney noted in his diary that although there was evidence of some slight improvement in business conditions, the "spirit of the business community is still despondent and inert." He wrote that he was "constantly informed" that everyone was waiting for the Royal Commission report and that no progress could be made in the country's affairs until it was received. In observing the scene he confirmed that while the anticipation of some form of commission may have been well-founded, nobody was certain as to the substantive content of the Commission's recommendations:

> Almost everyone I met speculated as to their findings and the effect they would have on business. Many conjectures were made but the Commission and the officials attached to it have wisely given no indication whatsoever as to their intentions. They have accomplished an extremely difficult task in a small place where rumour and conjecture are rife, and have gained the respect of the business community because of the manner in which they have conducted their enquiries and their ability in preventing any information leaking out concerning their report. [16]

UNTIL SUCH TIME

NOTWITHSTANDING THE RANGE of opinion that had developed in favour of some form of commission government, it is clear that right up to the moment the report was released on November 21st, there was no general expectation that it would recommend complete suspension of the institutions of responsible government. This is borne out by commentary in the press, and by remarks made by Gordon Bradley, the leader of the Liberal opposition in the House of Assembly. [17] Upon the release of the report, the *Telegram* and the *Daily News* embraced its recommendations without reservation. During the next several days, before the debate in the Assembly opened on November 27th, both papers urged its immediate adoption, without recourse to a referendum, and reported support for the report from the St. John's Board of Trade, the Great War Veterans Association, the Co-operative Self-Association of Harbour Grace, and others. [18] When the Assembly opened, it moved with great haste and little ceremony to accept in full the recommendations of the Royal Commission. In addition to the plan for meeting interest payments due on January 1st, these recommendations included the suspension of the "existing form of government...until such time as the Island may become self-supporting again," and the introduction of "a special Commission of Government" comprised of the Governor and six members, three from Newfoundland and three from Britain. [19]

In the "twofold character" of the report's recommendations, the measures to relieve the country of its financial burden, including the provision of substantial grants-in-aid, hardly needed exposition as they provided what everyone had hoped, an immediate solution to an intractable set of problems. But the report went to great lengths to justify its recommendations for changes to the political system. It described and explained many contributing factors which had produced what it called a "general demoralisation of the people." It said there was a "*vis inertiae*" existing throughout the country, resulting largely from the iniquitous credit system in the fishery and the "far-reaching psychological effects" this had created among the population. The account of the workings of this system was detailed and merciless in its indictment of the role of the merchants, particularly in their repeated failure to work co-operatively to overcome "jealousy and intrigue" and to establish the industry on a "rational and scientific basis." [20] The report followed this analysis with a discussion of the evidence it had received concerning the political system, and concluded that "as a general statement, it is not too much to say that the present generation of Newfoundlanders have never known enlightened government." (See

Appendix C.) The country had an annual deficit on its current account for twelve consecutive years and in the 1932-33 fiscal year, this was projected to rise to at least three million dollars, or forty per cent of the country's revenue. Total interest payments on annual borrowing, and on debts incurred from the war years and the operation of the railway now consumed sixty per cent of the country's revenue. [21] The combined effects of financial mismanagement and self-interest in both the political system and the fishery had put the country in an extremely vulnerable position, unable to withstand the devastating impact of the collapse in fish prices that began in 1930.

The report stated that by 1932 "no less than seventy thousand persons, or twenty-five per cent of the population were in receipt of public relief, other than poor relief or relief for the aged poor." Then, in 1933, any prospects for even a temporary recovery were destroyed as the inshore fishery collapsed, affecting "nearly three quarters of the population." [22] Finally, the Commissioners ventured to "emphasize" certain aspects of political life which deserved particular consideration and focused on two of these. The first concerned the issue of "job farming" and the effects of the "spoils system" on the administration of government. It noted that the small population of St. John's provided a limited pool from which to recruit an educated class for the civil service: "…The members of it are all known, if not related, to each other: everyone knows everyone else's business and it is a simple matter to ascertain which way any particular civil servant voted." [23] While such a picture may appear patronizing, this does not mean it was inaccurate. The report went on to examine the consequences of denominationalism on the workings of government. It drew the conclusion that instead of the churches playing a positive role as a "check to political malpractice," sectarian divisions only served to contribute to the "general de-moralization." [24]

All of this was used to construct a background analysis designed to establish a case for dismantling the country's political machinery as a means of securing its solvency. Aside from the sale of Labrador and the possibility of confederation—both rejected as not viable—three scenarios for political reform were put forward, options the report said represented the range of views submitted by witnesses. These were introduced with a statement of guiding principle: financial assistance would have to be coupled with far-reaching political changes that would advance not only "material prosperity," but also allow the country to "win free from the malign influences" that might otherwise threaten any prospects for recovery. The three scenarios outlined were: a continuation of the existing form of government with modifications to ensure permanent expenditure control; alterations to the system of government without modifying the constitution; and finally, a "radical change of system." [25]

These possibilities reflected the options in the September memorandum prepared by Clutterbuck. In the report, the first two were rejected in a perfunctory fashion as not meeting the test of providing a new political machinery that would "ensure the execution of a constructive forward policy designed to improve the condition of the people." Through a circular logic, the report's outcome was pre-determined by a condition which precluded certain potential options: "We are satisfied that such machinery could not be created without a modification of the existing constitution." The Commissioners concluded that they would not be justified in enlisting the financial assistance of the British government "while the fundamental causes of the present difficulties were to be neglected." Finally, the report made its case explicit in a statement that reflects both a self-conscious hesitation in offering its programme and the combined weight of arguments from witnesses and the British authorities for anti-democratic measures:

> After much anxious consideration, therefore, and in spite of a strong pre-disposition in favour of the maintenance of established institutions, we have been forced to the conclusion that only by a radical change of regime for a limited period of years can the Island be assisted to effective recovery. [26]

The report then gave consideration to two final possibilities: the formation of a National government or an extension of the existing parliament. Both of these were seen as inadequate to the desires of that "great majority of witnesses" who called for a rest from politics, and who differed only as to the form that rest might take:

> The desideratum was not that the country should be freed for the time being from the prospect of a general election, and from the demoralising influences of party politics, but that...the existing Legislative machine should be temporarily suspended and the government of the country placed for a period of years in the hands of a "Commission." [27]

This passage represents the formal introduction of the language Coaker had been using for eight years into the lexicon of constitutional discourse. It is made clear in the report that the concept which gave it definition was taken from the people who had made submissions to the Royal

Commission. It may be that there was some exaggeration in who, exactly, was counted among the estimate of the "great majority" in favour of this rest from politics. There was also no notice made of those who had made eloquent arguments about preserving, through democratic institutions, the sanctity of responsible government. The list of intervenors for and against commission government attached at the end of Clutterbuck's September memorandum contained a number of inaccuracies, and there were significant omissions from the tally sheet, but the errors cut both ways. Taylor from the Bank of Commerce was listed as "for" when his testimony indicates the opposite, and Cashin was shown as against, when according to the notes of the secretary he had conceded that commission might be the best option. [28] It was undoubtedly difficult to keep a scoresheet when both the variations on the options and the players themselves kept shifting position. But ultimately, as the reception to the report showed, there was no significant base of opposition to the proposed "radical change of regime."

The intervention in the House of Assembly by Liberal leader Gordon Bradley is notable in a number of respects. He admitted that he had "no knowledge whatsoever" as to the report's contents and though he had made a guess, he was "many, many miles from the truth." In introducing his remarks he articulated a defense of what he called the "sovereign rights" of a people under natural law, and said the population had "never dreamed," when electing the members to the House, that they would take away such rights without the consent of the people. He also expressed the view that the essential problem with the report was the failure of the Commissioners to penetrate "the company manner of witnesses" and to "get inside the skins of the great mass of individuals." As a result, he saw great danger in the effect the report would have on the people and the reaction over time to the absence of direct representation. [29]

He thus argued the main thrust of the critique put forward by Coaker, which was that the proposals contained the potential for provoking a popular revolt against the abrogation of the right of self-government. It is also clear that Coaker provided the basis for a series of amendments proposed by Bradley to establish a further process of review of the report, by sending a delegation to London to seek terms which would not involve the loss of representative institutions. Coaker issued an unsuccessful appeal for citizens to organize meetings and to petition for such action. [30] Bradley referred to a letter from Coaker published in the *Telegram* and reprinted in the *Advocate* (see Appendix E), and demanded accountability on Alderdice's campaign promise to investigate the commission idea, with action to be taken only upon the results of a plebiscite. [31]

As Prime Minister, and one of only a handful of speakers during the debate, Alderdice responded to Bradley by insisting that the Commissioners had indeed reflected the essential sentiments of the people: "It seems to be almost uncanny how [they] were able to enter into the minds of our people and paint such a truthful picture of our affairs." He took strong objection to Coaker's published analysis, and in particular, to the view that the country's status would be reduced to that of a Crown Colony, or in Coaker's words, the same type of government reserved for "coloured races." The Prime Minister indicated the governor would not be given any more authority than to follow the advice of the commissioners, and in his own uninspired turn of phrase, suggested this would place the country "betwixt and between a Crown Colony and a Dominion."

He then managed a rhetorical flourish in his concluding remarks, reciting a long list of those for whom he spoke, emphasizing the desperate plight of fishermen, loggers, miners—"workers of all classes" who were unemployed, and women and children "suffering from the pangs of hunger and cold." All such conditions, along with the uncertainties facing civil servants, teachers, and business-men, could only be addressed by accepting the new regime as proposed. Alderdice ended by thanking the British Government for a generous offer and proclaiming that on behalf of all Newfoundlanders, the government accepted the report "fully, frankly and freely." [32]

Bradley's amendments were presented in the spirit of closing arguments in a case already lost. He indicated that the Liberal party, at least what remained of it, would assist in the new scheme of government, and would not counte-nance a total rejection of the British offer. When his amendments were defeated, he and his colleague, R.J. Starkes, left their seats in the Assembly and the resolution to accept the report was adopted unanimously. [33] Bradley returned to the House two days later to participate in its indefinite suspension, seconding a motion put forward by Alderdice formally thanking the British Crown and assur-ing it of "the grateful and hearty co-operation of all patri-otic citizens." [34]

ACCUSING DEMOCRACY OF A CRIME

IT WAS SIGNIFICANT that the measures were approved in the Newfoundland Assembly without a recorded contrary vote. This made the task of pushing the required resolu-tions through the House of Commons that much easier for the British government. There, debate was much more extensively engaged. Though the outcome was never in question, many of England's most senior politicians participated in a number of sessions on an omnibus "Newfoundland Bill," including one all-night sitting which set a post-war record of twenty-three continuous hours of debate. [35]

The Labour opposition to Ramsay MacDonald's National government raised a number of issues opposing the report, which one of its leaders, future Prime Minister Clement Attlee, read as describing "an utter failure of competitive capitalism." In addition to placing unreasonable burdens on British taxpayers who were experiencing their own share of suffering, the report was seen to offer nothing that would address the "fundamental viciousness of the economic system" in Newfoundland. It merely proposed to bail out bondholders and hand the country "back to the capitalists." [36] The young Labour MP, Aneurin Bevan, demanded to know how it could be justified that the people themselves were not being consulted on the matter. Bevan insisted that neither the House of Commons, nor the government of Newfoundland had the authority to set aside Newfoundland's constitution for an indefinite period and to "abrogate the powers of the Newfoundland people." [37]

Stafford Cripps, another Labour MP, spoke directly to the question of the loss of democratic institutions, and denounced the proposals as reflecting a "tendency to accuse democracy of a crime for which it is not responsible." He particularly emphasized that the wording of the government's legislation provided for Newfoundland's Letters Patent to be "revoked" without any provision for their re-instatement, an unacceptable affront to the dignity of the population. [38] As a result of this intervention, J. H. Thomas, the Secretary of State, conceded that the government would amend the wording to read "suspend" when the legislation was sent for final approval to the House of Lords. [39] This, however, was not enough to win over the critics, who included the independent Liberal and former Prime Minister Lloyd George. The elder statesman of British politics "strongly objected" to providing assistance to the holders of Newfoundland stock when it was the people who were suffering, and insisted that any expenditure of funds should be made directly to the fishery and "those industries which represent the potential wealth of the island." [40] The Labour militant A. M. Maxton observed that the great lesson for the people of Newfoundland was in the report's note that there were only "two principal political parties in the Island." That fact, he felt, "should be taken out and written in letters of gold." [41]

THE CONSTITUTION IS DEAD

THE ADVOCATE HAD continued to denounce the entire exercise as it was played out in the Legislatures of both countries. It offered a sarcastic rejoinder to the wording amendment, an opinion which ultimately spoke to both the failure of the country and the perceived distortion of a constitutional prescription the paper had championed for so long:

> Our main point in referring to this is to draw our readers' attention to the fact that there is another word in the English dictionaries spelt "renege." In a particular sense the word is used in reference to a player in a game of cards who does not "play the game." It can be used in a general sense as well, and one standard dictionary explaining it in this sense says it can be used in referring

to "one who fails to comply with one's promise or obligation." The constitution of Newfoundland is dead. The
game is played and the people know who reneged. His
name is F. C. Alderdice. [42]

The *Advocate* and Coaker were among the very few
voices raised in opposition to the proposals in
Newfoundland. These interventions resonated with indig-
nant patriotism in the face of what was seen as a "huge
piece of treachery" carried out "in an ignoble fashion with
indecent haste." [43] But these objections could not have
constituted a serious challenge, coming as they did from
the long-time leading proponents of commission government. Richard Squires, who had not been heard in public
for some time, sent a telegram opposing the report to the
British Dominions Office, and A. B. Morine, the old Tory
war-horse now living in Canada, wrote two extremely critical letters to the Toronto *Globe* and copied them for publication in the *Advocate*. [44]

The *Telegram* dismissed this limited expression of opposition and trumpeted the broad support the report was
receiving, noting that there was no "cavilling" in response.
Predictably, the *Daily News* charged Coaker with hypocrisy, with one columnist referring to him as the one who
had "made the welkin ring" promoting the commission
idea for years, now ungrateful and intemperate in his criticism. [45] The game was played and the constitution, for a
time at least, was indeed dead for all meaningful purposes.
In their rush to assign blame for what they saw as selling
out the country, Coaker and the *Advocate* appeared entirely oblivious to their essential contribution in setting the
stage for the final act.

Throughout this drama, the Amulree Royal Commission emerges front and centre as the primary vehicle for

the acting out of the country's conflicted political personality. As though in the image of the Amulree hearings, the
country was able to see a projection of its own future. The
real impact of the Royal Commission may have been that
by its very existence it offered a model of that elusive
arrangement which Coaker had been trying to define for
many years. In the process of the country's dialogue with
Amulree, a paradigm emerged that would simply involve
the transfer of authority from one Commission to another.
After all, it would not require much in the way of a radical
departure to go from entrusting a body of experts with the
troublesome task of charting a course for the future to
handing over the entire administration of the country to a
similar body with a mandate extended indefinitely. It is
perhaps fitting, then, that it was Coaker, the country's one
political actor who most clearly articulated a certain vision
of the future, who was also the most adamant in rejecting
the work of its harbinger.

Coaker was wrong when he predicted the population
would not stand for unilateral suspension of the country's
political institutions. The people did not respond to his
appeals for mobilization, nor spontaneously register any
discernible protest. This may be seen as a vindication of
the British decision to recommend proceeding without any
provision for broad consultation. While addressing the
urgency of a solution for imminent default on debt payments, the strategy of foregoing a referendum was not a big
risk in view of the enormous convergence of opinion
around the basic proposition that the political process itself
had to be usurped as a pre-condition for moving the country forward. Coaker again found himself in the familiar
position of denouncing a merchant government for selling
out the country, precisely the vantage point in 1925 which

first led him to call for the abolition of the party system of government. The Liberals may have been the only group willing to sponsor reform of the fishery, much needed as Amulree confirmed, but were otherwise incapable of governing responsibly. They were replaced at regular intervals by a merchant party dedicated to the self-interest of the business class. These "ins and outs" held the country back, producing continuous turmoil and endless intrigue without achieving a minimum level of political stability. For twenty years following the re-election of the Morris government in 1913, no political formation had been successful in winning a second term in office.

Positioning himself somewhere between a warning and a prediction, Coaker, in 1925 and periodically in the years that followed, offered a prescriptive remedy designed with the best of intentions. Its mission, however, was practically impossible: to reconcile a virtually unresolveable tension between preserving democratic practice and transforming traditional parliamentary institutions into an experimental and wholly unrecognizable form. To Coaker's credit, as his proposal for a commission form of government entered the realm of public consideration, he and the editorialists at the *Advocate* maintained a determined commitment to insist on the inviolable principle of representation as a necessary feature of political reform.

But inherent weaknesses in the idea gave rise to formidable obstacles blocking a clear vision toward its implementation. In *Advocate* editorials the formulation evolved from an initial suggestion of a commission composed of ten members, to one comprising nine, then six and finally three. Representatives were to be elected on denominational lines, which may have been a valid attempt to construct a new formula rooted in historical practice, but this was hardly a programme that would guarantee either representative or effective government. It was also entirely unclear how such a system could be efficiently introduced on the promise of a party coming to power with an intention to implement such a platform. A new government would first have to hold a referendum, on the assumption that it had no mandate to move unilaterally. If the results were favourable it would pass legislation to govern the holding of new elections contested by candidates whose only affiliation was religious. If the commission idea was supposed to minimize and eventually eliminate partisan conflict, it is difficult to see how such a process could have been carried out, particularly within a condensed time frame, without engendering a great deal of conflict in which sectarian and other interests substituted for political divisions, with no fewer complicating and debilitating consequences.

As it turned out, the ascension to power of Alderdice's party in 1932 and the subsequent appointment of the Amulree Commission, with its process of consultation, was as close to being true to Coaker's programme as could be realistically expected. Here another defect in the proposal was revealed. The critical issue of implementation was entrusted (and quite consciously so, in Coaker's recruitment of Alderdice to the idea) to a merchant regime that lacked a fundamental commitment to democratic values. Coaker's proposal would, given the turns of the political wheel, almost inevitably come to rest with a party guided by that ancient instinct of restricting the perceived evils of popular rule.

Following the election of Alderdice, the country sank deeper into the abyss of financial disaster, and the commission idea gained increasing adherents through public debate in the capital city among those preoccupied with seeking solutions to the unfolding national emergency. But in many of the submissions made to the Royal Commission by leading merchants, in much of the pro-government press commentary, and in the closing speech of Alderdice in the House of Assembly—in none of these places was there a professed commitment to democratic principles approaching anything like that articulated by Coaker. Notwithstanding his own career as a populist leader with an autocratic bent and some evidence of unmistakeably anti-democratic impulses—as for example, when he called for a Mussolini-like solution to impose regulations on the fish merchants in the fall of 1932—Coaker's interventions on the extremely troubling issues of the day were generally not of a facile kind. [46] While he was advocating a dramatic change to the political system and struggled to maintain a vision that would see it retain representative features, others took his idea and promoted a transparently undemocratic structure of an appointed committee as a substitute for responsible government. The final momentum came from the British perception of an existing public consensus in Newfoundland regarding the basic question of eliminating the political game altogether from the business of administering the state.

Despite the absence of any mechanisms of accountability in its recommendations, the substantial content of the Commission's political analysis could have been authored by William Coaker at any time between 1925 and 1933. The evidence presented to the Royal Commission reflected a political discourse of the day in Newfoundland which framed the general crisis of the state as more than an economic one. A prevalent malaise lent itself very neatly to an agenda of the most conservative kind being fashioned in the Mother country. It is hard not to conclude that paranoid and fearful money managers in the British treasury overstated the case in their rather fanciful view of the importance of Newfoundland to the credit of the Empire. But in the final analysis, there was an undeniable political dimension to the country's "situation and prospects" which had been clearly manifest for some time. In the record of how Newfoundlanders themselves viewed the dire circumstances of their beseiged homeland, it may be seen that the radical solution brought forward by the Royal Commission served as an indirect expression of self-determination on behalf of a people who had shown themselves willing to yield their own voice.

The Newfoundland legislature was prorogued on Dec. 2nd, 1933. Albert Perlin wrote in the *Evening Telegram* that, save for selfish politicians and a few sentimentalists, there would be "none to shed a tear" for the final adjournment of the national parliament in the lifetime of many of the country's people. "Sentiment," he wrote, "is a pretty thing and I would not decry it, but we have passed the stage in our affairs when it must guide our actions." Perlin went on to suggest that the change in the system of government was not an end to the country's independence, but a beginning. He then enumerated the many ways in which the country had not been independent for some time. These included the effects of numerous examples of misgovernment: the long history of reckless borrowing, the wastage of resources, patronage in the civil service, the railroading of harmful legislation in spite of public disapproval, a loss of self-sufficiency among the people, and their dependence on the paternalism of government. He identified the greatest loss of independence as having been historically forged in the political game: "the whims and fancies, the hates or favours of men, some of whom were honest, a few competent, but most of them animated by personal ambitions and ready, in the furtherance of these ambitions, to ride roughshod over the liberties of the people." As an alternative to this, he suggested it would be a refreshing change to be governed by "experts imbued with the British tradition." Perlin's rather elaborate justification for the Amulree recommendations would later stand in direct contradiction to the memory he would invoke of this defining national moment.

ON REQUEST FROM THE
PEOPLE OF NEWFOUNDLAND

THE NEW COMMISSION of Government regime was sworn in at a ceremony at the Newfoundland Hotel on February 14th, 1934. Presided over by the governor, the occasion saw the introduction of three British commissioners to an august gathering of St. John's dignitaries, which included Alderdice and two of his ministers as the three Newfoundland commissioners. The early period of commission government saw only sporadic political activity in opposition to the new regime, largely led by the unemployed and poor of St. John's, who had continued their campaigns of direct action in the face of terrible conditions of poverty and destitution.

In May of 1935 another dramatic confrontation at the Colonial Building followed a large march of the city's unemployed, who had been organizing around demands concerning relief work and the administration of the dole. On this occasion, a re-organized and expanded police force was successful in routing the protesters. In the aftermath, quick action was taken to arrest four of the leaders of the unemployed movement, although they were eventually acquitted of all charges. James Overton has shown the political dimension of this unrest as both a deliberate challenge to the authority of the commission regime, and a pivotal event in establishing the resolve of the commissioners to stand fast in the face of what could be regarded as isolated resistance to their rule. Pierce Power, the most colourful leader among the unemployed, who had been deported from Canada for subversive activity, articulated a critique of the commission with both a clear sense of patriotic duty and a specific loyalty to his own class:

> "It is now...a contest between dictators and the masses of toiling Newfoundlanders trying to exist in their own country as decent human beings—a contest for right, justice and liberty between the proletariat and the oligarchy sent across the Atlantic to rule us against our will." [1]

CHAINED TO HEAVEN

IN CONTRAST TO such angry and politicized voices, the commission went about its business mindful of the need to appear responsive to local sensibilities, but determined to forge ahead with the burdensome challenge of providing sound administration in the absence of any outlet for the expression of political sentiment, subversive or otherwise. In the recently published correspondence of one of the first of the British commissioners, Sir John Hope Simpson, and his wife Quita, there is a vast collection of material revealing an unreconstructed colonial mentality in their opinions on the Newfoundland climate, both political and seasonal. Hope Simpson dismissed the organizing efforts of the unemployed and took pride in the increased efficiency of the police. "They were looked upon under the last regime as beneath contempt...now the whole of the mob has a very wholesome respect for the police, and the town (St. John's) feels very much happier than it did." [2] Unfortunately for the local merchant elite, Hope Simpson did not limit his disdain to unemployed agitators. He and his wife shared the views of the Amulree Commission in their hostility toward the selfish behaviour of the country's business class:

> "The merchants are incorrigible...living in luxury and driving motorcars (while) the fisherman is starving and has no decent clothes. 'Starving' is an exaggeration, but the standard of life is lower than anything you can find in Europe. It makes one realize how the love of money is the root of evil." [3]

These letters provide a fascinating study of the view behind what was most of the time a faceless regime, removed from the vagaries of competing demands for its attention. They also show that, despite the instances of mutual contempt between the bureaucratic rulers and their subjects, there were significant soft spots on both sides, as the Hope Simpsons travelled around the country and were for the most part greeted warmly wherever they went. The letters of Quita, especially, are a mix of patronizing hand-wringing about the lack of self-sufficiency among the poor combined with genuine shock and outrage at their conditions, and anger at the culpability of the country's elite. She also, in the tradition of the colonial observer, had a fine way with descriptive detail, particularly when it came to the unique climactic ambience, and the associated charms of the country's landscapes:

> This country is more colourful than Scotland; the atmosphere is so intensely clear that all the outlines and colours spring sharp cut and intensely vivid to the eye, so that the beauty catches you by the throat. And it is so intensely green and the sea and sky so deeply blue. And in addition there is here that quality of light you find in Greece—an indescribable radiance of dawn and sunset. You will think I exaggerate; I only tell you my

experience. Every day I am here I seem to feel the beauty of this country more intensely. There is an old story that the only people who have to be chained to heaven are the Newfoundlanders; they always want to get back to their island. [4]

Newfoundland during the Depression was not, of course, a very heavenly place. By the time of the approach of war at the end of the thirties, there were increasing calls for a return to self-government. Voices were roused following the publication of a small book by another of the first British Commissioners, Thomas Lodge, which assailed the workings of the commission as a dictatorship without redeeming merit. [5] These were overtaken by the fact of Newfoundland's critically important strategic location to the Allied powers. As Britain used its commissioners in negotiations with Canada and the U.S. to allow the full deployment of Newfoundland's resources to secure all possible military preparation for the defense of North America, the local population, with few exceptions, was too busy enjoying an economic boom to pay much attention to the constitutional niceties of the country's position. One of the exceptions was Joe Smallwood who, like Peter Cashin, had been involved in various attempts to resurrect political debate, calling for the commission experiment to come to an end. [6]

As is well known, Smallwood, until he became a pig farmer living off the proceeds of the Canadian air base in Gander, had a career as an itinerant journalist, broadcaster and follower of Liberal politicians during the 1920's. He had learned to believe in socialism studying with George Grimes, an FPU politician and intellectual, and had written first a pamphlet and then a book on William Coaker, claiming Coaker as Newfoundland's greatest son. [7]

Smallwood had gone off to New York and London where he was enthralled with the great socialist movements of those cities, but eventually returned home and sided with the less complicated opportunism of the Liberal party. He was then involved peripherally in its momentous decline, having been at Squires' side in the Colonial Building during the riot of 1932, and defeated as a Liberal candidate in the election that spring. Smallwood later claimed to have told the voters of the Bonavista district during this, the only unsuccessful campaign of his career, not to bother voting because "I guarantee you here and now that inside of two years the House of Assembly will be closed down, the government will be turned out, and Newfoundland will be under a Royal Commission appointed by the King." [8] Smallwood's uncorroberated and counterfactual accounts of history notwithstanding—he also wrote that he had been thrown out of the merchant's meeting on the eve of the riot, when in fact the meeting he'd been tossed out of occurred a year earlier [9] —his involvement in the political events of this period left a permanent mark that would come to shape both his own future and the destiny of the country when the war ended.

By the end of the war the political position, and therefore the viability, of the commission regime had become very untenable. Public opinion converged in opposition to the actions taken by the commission government when it legislated a series of shameless violations of Newfoundland's territorial integrity by granting leases to American and Canadian governments for the land on which their bases were built. Peter Neary has shown that the second of these agreements involving the transfer of the base at Goose Bay in Labrador to Canada generated the most opposition and the rising of a nationalist sentiment, particularly among the St. John's elite. [10] This agreement was in fact only a scaled down version of a more significant precedent which had been set with the Americans earlier in the war when they were granted ninety-nine year leases to land in Argentia, Stephenville and St. John's, as part of an Anglo-American deal. The U.S. gave the British navy a fleet of destroyers in return for a proprietry claim to their bases in Newfoundland. The recurring placement of Newfoundland's sovereignty as a pawn in the political relationships of larger powers highlighted the reality for the people that their country was not their own.

THE NATIONAL CONVENTION
AND HISTORICAL MEMORY

IN MARCH 1946, on the eve of the election of delegates to the national convention called to discuss Newfoundland's constitutional future, Albert Perlin was now writing the lead column in the *Daily News* under the byline "Wayfarer." At this point, prior to the emotional fireworks that would soon be underway in the Colonial Building, he expressed a general concern about the limited scope of the convention's advisory role to the British government. Anxious about the quality of historical knowledge on the loss of self-government in 1933 that existed among the people, and among those campaigning for election to the convention, Perlin wrote:

> The new voters have small knowledge of the past. Many of them have wholly distorted viewpoints for which they cannot be blamed. It is always convenient to find a scapegoat for our own faults and those who were voters prior to the commission era have not only laid on the heads of politicians the blame these should accept,

but have also made them responsible for popular short-comings. When the younger generation has asked why we no longer have responsible government, their elders say with almost a single voice: because we had wicked politicians who were as incompetent as they were corrupt. This is a sad commentary upon our understanding of the past. [11]

This is the same Perlin who deliberately focused on precisely such wickedness in 1933. During the upheaval which accompanied the winding down of the operation of government by commission, Perlin was not alone in attempting to construct a view of the past which denied the complicity of so many, including himself, in the country's loss of nationhood. Among the forty delegates elected to the national convention in the spring of 1946, only three had previously been elected to sit in the Assembly at the Colonial Building, now being brought back to centre stage following an ignominious term in which it housed the offices of the commission regime. Peter Cashin, Gordon Bradley (the last Liberal leader), and Ken Brown (the country's first Minister of Labour, appointed by Alderdice after he deserted the Liberals in 1932) would all figure prominently in the two-year run-up to the referendum campaigns in the summer of 1948. Along with Perlin, these men and others such as Smallwood, carried forward an uncertain continuity between the generations, one they tried to shape to suit their own interests as they re-inhabited the vacant political space which had been occupied by the experiment in government by commission. In the bridging of the historical memory from one defining national moment to another, there was a fundamental disagreement on the meaning of the common reference points that constituted the past. While such differences may have been in part self-serving, they were also an expression of the country's inherited and disorienting dependence on the perpetually guiding hand of the Mother country.

Clement Atlee was now the Prime Minister in Britain, the first Labour leader to have achieved an outright electoral majority by defeating Winston Churchill in 1945. Peter Clutterbuck, secretary to the Amulree Commission, had been appointed High Commissioner to Canada. Together, along with others such as Aneurin Bevan and numerous bureaucrats who had been party to the Newfoundland debates in 1933 and during the commission government, these British officials had their own reference points in relation to Newfoundland, and not surprisingly, their own agenda.

In December, 1945 Atlee announced in the House of Commons that a national convention would be called in Newfoundland "to consider and discuss...the changes that have taken place in the financial and economic situation of the Island since 1934...and to make recommendations to His Majesty's government as to possible forms of future government to be put before the people at a national referendum." [12] It is clear from the diplomatic records prior to and after this declaration, that while the British government was moving toward defining its own interest as one that would see Newfoundland joining with Canada, Atlee and others responsible for this policy were preparing for any eventuality, including the restoration of full responsible government. [13] The problem with the announcement, and this provided the key rallying cry for what would become the anti-confederate forces, was that the resolutions passed in 1933 by the Newfoundland Assembly had clearly stated in their petition to the British Crown that new Letters Patent should be issued to provide for the country's administration "until such time as it may become self-supporting again." The legislation passed in Britain was written "to make provision for the administration of Newfoundland on the basis of the recommendations of the Royal Commission." And the original starting point for the actions of both legislatures, the Amulree recommendations, were clear:

> "It would be understood that, as soon as the Island's difficulties are overcome and the country is again self-supporting, responsible government, on request from the people of Newfoundland, would be restored." [14]

Atlee's announcement in 1945 outlined a process that would generate advisory recommendations to the British government, rather than moving directly to restoration of responsible government. Newfoundland's unprecedented prosperity in an era of full employment brought about by the base-building boom undertaken by the American and Canadian governments, had generated increasing calls for the immediate restoration of self-government. The country's financial position was indeed a self-supporting one, and Attlee's speech was seen by many as a violation of the undertakings made in 1933.

In the national convention poll, Joe Smallwood was elected as a delegate from Gander in the riding of Bonavista Centre. Following the announcement that the commission would sponsor the calling of such a political assembly, he had immediately come to the conclusion that the central issue facing the country must be defined as whether to enter the Canadian federation, and had begun promoting this option before the convention's first sitting. It has been frequently noted that many people, including numerous delegates, were shocked when what was expected to be a fairly neutral undertaking to "consider and discuss" the country's economic and constitutional position was very quickly hijacked by Smallwood's efforts to force the debate in the direction of confederation. [15] While this may have been the case, the convention had already witnessed a spectacular grandstanding effort when Peter Cashin rose for the first time in his place to denounce the calling of the convention as an unacceptable affront to the people and a violation of the promised return to responsible government. In so doing, Cashin had picked up almost precisely where he left off in 1932, invoking in the most flamboyant rhetoric the image of the screaming political debates which had precipitated the final loss of faith in the country's democratic institutions.

Cashin heaped scorn on top of invective against all manner of British involvement in the country's affairs, and specifically reviewed the Amulree report as the beginning of this unwarranted and unwanted interference. He alleged that "a gun was put to our heads, the demand that we first commit political suicide before any assistance would be forthcoming." In a classic case of revisionism and selective memory which would have a lasting influence in creating a distorted view of the Amulree process as nothing other than a poorly disguised British plot, he elaborated his point:

> The (Amulree) report says that Newfoundland was led to ask for assistance from the United Kingdom. I contend the word "led" is not accurate. It should have read we were mercilessly dragged and driven into the pit prepared for us. And above all, this report completely ignores the fact that the Alderdice government with whom they were dealing was acting in callous violation

of its election pledges; that the whole thing was dripping with treachery and broken faith, and that the British government was fully aware that it was dealing with leaders who had been traitors to their country and who were agents acting without any legal authority. [16]

In the interest of establishing unquestionable certainty concerning Newfoundland's right to retrieve its lost status, Cashin, like Perlin, conveniently obliterated from the historical record his own personal contribution to the shaping of the Amulree report. Not only had he told the Commissioners a commission form of government might be desirable, but his own prior behaviour as one of the country's leading political figures contributed to the general mistrust of the population toward politicians that gave Amulree the commission idea in the first place. Like Coaker at the time of the adoption of the Amulree report, Cashin was desperately setting out to alter the record after the fact, as though he were innocent of any of its implications. In the months that followed this intervention, he reiterated numerous times in the debates this view of the Amulree report and eventually extended it to allege that the first Newfoundland commissioners, appointed from Alderdices' cabinet, had accepted bribes in exchange for their support of the report. [17] This resulted in a libel suit against him which was dismissed without a verdict ever being reached by the jury. [18]

Cashin was also, at this early stage of the convention, laying down a conspiracy theory that he would maintain over the course of the drama about to unfold during the next two years. His was the mantle of the self-appointed patriot (a decorated Major no less), determined to the bitter end to see in every battle lost, and finally in the last ballot results the war itself, as the handiwork of unscrupulous forces aligned in the singular purpose of denying Newfoundland her natural right of self-determination. This vision won many supporters at the time and continues to reverberate down to the present. What it does not take account of is the fact that these outside forces were, in the confederation struggle, as in the debacle of 1933, wholly dependent for the success of any such malevolent designs on the willing co-operation of some significant portion of the Newfoundland people themselves, and not incidentally, of their political leadership.

GROUNDED IN LESSONS LEARNED

MANY DELEGATES TO the national convention, even those who would come to actively campaign against confederation, were appalled at the bitter and violent language of Cashin's speeches, and rejected outright his assertions about the intentions of the British government. Charles Bailey, a fisherman and sailor elected from Trinity South, was one of only a couple of organizers sent to the outports by the Responsible Government League. [19] He said he was strongly committed to responsible government and described himself as having been a "left-wing socialist since 1910" who had travelled "to nearly every country with a coastline in the world." Bailey took great objection to Cashin's attempt to discredit the actions of Attlee's government. "The only chance for the Labour party to find out if there was any political talent and interest in government was to call a national convention. Take it from me, Labour is in sympathy with us and don't put the blame on them. " [20]

Ken Brown, who after serving in Alderdice's cabinet became president of a much weakened FPU in 1935, was also a strong anti-confederate. He provided one of the most dramatic moments of the convention when he collapsed from a brain hemorrage during a passionate speech denouncing Smallwood. He responded to Cashin's inflammatory remarks by saying that he was the only person present in the Assembly who had voted for the Amulree report and that he was not ashamed of this, because it was a choice of "voting out responsible government" or "letting 70,000 men, women and children in this country starve." Brown offered a defense of the commission government and pointed to the good things it had done for the people, particularly in advancing the rights of labour and trade unions. He also said that if a vote were taken among the fishermen, eighty-five per cent would support commission government, as "this is the only form of government that ever did anything for the fishermen." [21]

It is noteworthy that virtually all the delegates elected from labour backgrounds to the convention were strongly in favour of a return to responsible government. This is particularly so in light of the fact that Smallwood eventually ran the two referendum campaigns in 1948 with an organization that some referred to as a gang of "bolsheviks." [22] Through the course of most of the convention proceedings there was no clear demarcation of opinion or debate along class lines. Larger national issues were at stake, involving the very definition of the country's basic interests. But by the time the convention was drawing to a close in January of 1948, it was clear that the coming referendum battles would partly be fought as something of a class conflict, as Smallwood intensified his efforts to proseletize on the constitutional issue by constantly attacking the privileges of the Water Street merchants. Although their interests were represented in the Assembly by the likes of Ches Crosbie, the son of the former Finance

Minister and others, it was Cashin who took the lead in linking the country's welfare to that of its merchants. He said that as he listened to one of Smallwood's speeches he realized a threatening spectre was present:

> ...for the first time a new and unsavoury and even alien note (has) been injected into the proceedings of this convention. It seemed to me that a foreign influence was loose: the spirit of Trotsky, the virulent harangue of the soap-box orator playing on the discontent of an unthinking and innocent people.[23]

For his part, Smallwood had by this time waged a very successful campaign to control and dominate the focus of debate. He developed a number of themes that together represented a very sophisticated appeal to the population of the country as it listened to the convention proceedings broadcast on their radio sets. Smallwood pitched his elaborately detailed sermons on the benefits of confederation not to the immediate forces arrayed against him in the chamber, but directly via the airwaves to the toiling masses and their families. It was clear from the beginning that the significant majority of delegates would be persuaded of only one thing, and this was the position being constantly argued by Perlin in his columns—that whatever else might occur in the future, the country should first regain its lost status as an independent nation. For many, including Perlin, this did not necessarily mean that the issue of confederation would not be placed before the people at some point in the future. On the contrary, the only correct way for Newfoundland to join Canada was to negotiate entry as an agreement between two equal nations. It would seem the country had reverted to a position where it was now appropriate for it to be guided by that principle which

Perlin had derided in 1933, namely a certain "sentiment" concerning the inviolability of independence.

On this question, Smallwood had a different analysis from most of the leading players on the stage, with the notable exception of Bradley. As the second chairman of the convention, Bradley became the other primary instrument for advancing the confederate cause. Along with his role in the convention, his outspoken defense of independence in 1933 would have placed him in a unique position where he was the last who could be accused of being a quisling. Grounded in the lessons learned from their own personal experience in the country's earlier failure, for Bradley and Smallwood the prospect of an immediate return to responsible government did not hold out the promise of a constitutional status most likely to ensure a rehabilitation of the country's dignity. Smallwood spoke directly to the presumption that what had once been the source of national honour and pride should serve again as the model for the future:

> Our danger, so it seems to me, is that of nursing delusions of grandeur. We remember stories of small states that valiantly preserved their national independence and developed their own proud cultures, but we tend to overlook the fact that comparison of Newfoundland with them is ludicrous. We are not a nation. We are merely a medium sized municipality, a mere miniature borough of a large city…There was indeed a time when tiny states lived gloriously. That time is now ancient European history. We are trying to live in the mid-20th century, post-Hitler new world. We are living in a world in which small countries have less chance than ever before of surviving. [24]

This speech was delivered in the context of proposing a motion to send a delegation to Ottawa to seek discussions on possible terms of union with Canada. While defining rather boldly Smallwood's assessment of how Newfoundland should think of itself, this analysis was a complete contradiction of his boosterism and hyperbole from an earlier moment when he saw a country that would take its place among the "great small nations of the world." [25] As events unfolded, those in the convention who were not disposed toward confederation gave their support to Smallwood's motion in the interests of a balanced investigation of all possible options. In doing so, they provided him the opportunity to return to the convention with a fully developed set of proposals on confederation. A delegation would also be sent to London, to clarify the position of Britain on the financial and other arrangements for the return of responsible government. This delegation was met with a parsimonious and generally unfriendly welcome, a signal that there could be no assumptions about any straightforward move in this direction. Britain and Canada were clearly working hand in hand to facilitate the emergence of confederation as the most attractive option. Canada was motivated largely by counteracting the influence of the U.S. on its doorstep, but was also pursuing some Canadian version of manifest destiny, in seeking to extend its reach to the eastern edge. Britain was increasingly consumed by the process of decolonization occuring throughout the empire. Its interests were plainly defined by the need to disengage from Newfoundland without incurring further responsibility for the country's affairs, political or financial.

Ultimately the final decision was going to be Newfoundland's, and all parties understood this. The only undetermined issue was the options on which the people would be consulted. When the national convention concluded its business by rejecting a resolution from Smallwood to include confederation on the referendum ballot along with the options of continuing government by commission or returning to responsible government, the British government took decisive action. It rejected the convention's advice, instead announcing that the forthcoming referendum would contain all three options. Smallwood had taken to the airwaves and launched a massive petition campaign denouncing the "twenty-nine dictators" who had voted against his motion, and calling on the people to express their support for a chance to vote on confederation. Though there were complaints of conspiratorial designs against Newfoundland's democratic will as expressed by the convention, the British initiative was entirely consistent with both its own desire to ensure a fair hearing for confederation, and the fundamental principle that the direct voice of the people had yet to be heard from. Smallwood was on the side of the angels, arguing that it was not credible to maintain that the people had no right to pass judgement on what had clearly become a serious option with substantial popular support. Given that one of the biggest grievances about the introduction of commission government had been the absence of a referendum in 1933, this was no time to circumscribe the choices to be put to the people.

A SAFE HARBOUR

THE STORY OF the two referendum campaigns has been told and re-told, with no shortage of literary license or eyewitness dramatization. Smallwood and his supporters carried the day on the second vote by a margin that was very close, yet not exactly razor thin—almost five percentage points, or just less than 7,000 votes out of a total of 149,667, across twenty-five districts. [26] This victory was based on a dramatic geographic divide. The seven losing districts that produced a majority for responsible government were all located on the Avalon peninsula in the proximity of St. John's. It has been commonly noted that this division ran parallel to a religious polarization that arose through the provocation of the Catholic Church, which played a leading role in articulating a nationalist sentiment in opposition to any action other than a return to responsible government. This view, rooted in an unwavering hostility to perceived forces of secularization, found a receptive base among the working class of St. John's, who once again, as they had historically, lined up with the largely Protestant merchant elite to oppose an outport-led initiative. It has also been noted that the further away the voters were from St. John's, the less likely they were to identify with a "national" project whose interests, as they always had been, would remain dominated by the capital. There is also no doubt that in the choice of wording on the ballot, "Responsible Government, as it existed in 1933," the British successfully conjured an image of the past which reminded people of the down side of independence, the deeply resented, largely corrupt and fundamentally unstable political machine which had not proven itself capabable of advancing the country's basic interests.

The anti-confederate forces, and many of those who continue to identify with the lost cause of independence, have maintained a variety of spurious charges over the years that the vote was somehow fixed. Specific instances of vote tampering have been alleged but never proven. Presumably to account for the fact that such corruption would have had to occur on a massive scale with most of the country asleep, one conspiracy theory with some prominence (a version of it popularized by the feature film *Secret Nation*) alleges that the vote totals were switched—which of course makes no sense in light of the outcome as reported and published by district—and the results were really the opposite of what was reported. None of these notions have any real credibility, but they have entered the domain of folklore, and continue to evoke a lasting and haunting dimension in an unresolved contest, forever casting doubt on the legitimacy of a fateful decision. The most substantial challenge to the result of the vote is the suggestion that the country was profoundly divided, and on such a significant constitutional issue, a greater majority of opinion should have been required. Maybe so.

The fact is the rules were clear to everyone and following the first campaign, there was never any question of anything other than a simple majority governing the outcome. Joe Smallwood had presented to the country a package of proposals from Canada that he and the delegation from the national convention had negotiated as draft Terms of Union. He proceeded to campaign on these as a promise of prosperity drawn in a colourful and compelling social democratic hue. The beneficence of the Canadian welfare state represented a tremendously hopeful prospect to a people for whom adversity was a way of life. Smallwood spoke directly to the people of the outports, often in language lifted directly from the great orations of William Coaker. In the first referendum the strongest support for the option of continuing government by commission was among the northern districts most loyal to Coaker's Fishermen's Protective Union with twenty-six per cent in Fogo and forty-two per cent in

Twillingate respectively. In the drive to secure a majority on the second ballot, Smallwood out-organized the competition in a masterful mobilization of energy and political smarts. What had been for so long the country's St. John's ruling class simply could not keep up, as the lopsided majorities for responsible government in the capital were outnumbered by smaller margins for confederation much more numerous elsewhere.

Cashin, Crosbie and the young Don Jamieson, later to become Pierre Trudeau's external affairs minister, split among themselves into two groups, one calling for economic union with the United States and the other appealing to the natural and longstanding patriotic sentiment of keeping the Canadian wolf at bay. In their disorganized attempt to appropriate the language and symbols of the country's heritage as their own, they were outwitted by a band of activists who had decided on a different expression of loyalty to their beloved homeland. No less dedicated and righteous than their adversaries, the confederate mission was to save the country from the designs of Water Street merchants by bringing it to a safe harbour in the protection of the Canadian federation. In their wisdom, however tentative the resolve, the people of Newfoundland said no to the option that represented the most likely return to opportunism and failure. It was obviously not an easy thing to do, for in the bargain they had to forego a chance to revisit sovereign independence, which after all, still carried the enormous weight of sentiment, if not any guarantees of much else.

The game continues

If it can be fairly said that for Newfoundland confederation was a good idea, it would not be too much of a stretch to say that it was just about the only good idea Joe Smallwood had. Shortly after being sworn in as the new province's first premier, having been so designated by Canadian Prime Minister Louis St. Laurent amid a constitutional uncertainty that simply would not stand in the way of the victor getting his spoils, Smallwood nominated Helena Squires, the country's first female politician, as president of the Newfoundland Liberal party. [27] It was a transparent attempt to resurrect and whitewash the memory of the supposedly once-great Liberal Prime Minister. In the first federal election campaign following his own election as premier, Smallwood proceeded to unearth the most contemptible political practices from the past and directly threatened a group of voters on the southern shore of the Avalon peninsula with dire consequences if they did not support his candidate. [28] After his candidate lost, he was taken to court for violating the elections law, but clearly came to learn nothing about containing his arrogance or presumptive powers. Electoral politics appeared to resume as though the failure of the country in 1933 and the intervening commission experiment were minor and insignificant interruptions in the normal base conduct of the affairs of state.

In 1950, Peter Clutterbuck visited Newfoundland and wrote one last thoughtful memo on this file, in which he expressed a certain wonder and a little awe at the changes coming over the place. He reported that Smallwood had confided in him that the new province was a perfect laboratory for the working out of what the Premier called a "democratic dictatorship." [29] This vision was one evidently based on raising the old habits of political intrigue and manipulation to new heights, and combining these with the newly-imprinted methods of modern government established during the dictatorship of the commission. Grand and magnificent schemes were unabashedly promoted as monument-building exercises in the service of Smallwood's ego and then launched through a preposterous parade of charlatans and con artists from away. There was also, of course, no shortage of local call on the available resources of the public treasury. It was not long before many of Smallwood's most ardent and able supporters in the confederation battle left his side, and he in turn began to desert the people who had made him their leader. By the time of his assault on the rights of trade unions during the woodworkers' strike of 1959, [30] Smallwood had become a gross caricature of those players of political gamesmanship who had gone before him, and who never seemed able to rise to a calling greater than that of their own self-aggrandizement and preservation.

Despite a modest few achievements and no end of bragging rights about them, Smallwood went on to become a great embarrassment and a terrible liability to Newfoundland. He did nothing to rehabilitate politics and did many things to bring it once again into general disrepute. Remarkably, like Squires, he sustained an incredible ability to regenerate himself and win the support of those who could claim to be the best and brightest in the small town politics of St. John's. After a decade or so as a province of Canada, at a time when the whole world began to convulse politically, yet another generation of Liberals came of age, and in Newfoundland they clamoured for positioning at Smallwood's side. Crosbie, Cashin, Hickman, Wells, Roberts, Rowe, Neary, Jamieson—echoing in this roll call could be heard the political ambitions of previous generations. While not all this new crowd stayed with Smallwood, many of them did persist through his most ridiculous excesses. The game, alas, was continuing, as it would for twenty-two years before Smallwood was finally removed from office. In the light of his tenure, it is perhaps understandable that the view of confederation as having been a great mistake did not totally diminish with time.

For those who still seek clarity on this fateful event, not for the sake of judging the past but in the interest of constructing a more far-sighted perspective, the decision to join Canada really only makes sense in the context of a longer view which connects it to the prior crisis of an earlier day. William Coaker never did reform the fishery. It was the commission government and its professionalized methods of governance that established the first comprehensive state regulation of the industry. The ultimate loss of faith in Newfoundland's democratic institutions in 1932-33 was one local strain, not so virulent as others in the world at the time, of collective despondency in the face of overwhelming odds and obstacles. And while the story of this previous era is not a pleasant one, as we can see from the various efforts of those who were there to embellish and re-fashion it, there is no escaping ownership of those events. Newfoundland in the depths of the Depression may have been in the grip of forces beyond its control, but the political solution that was offered for its problems was not something dreamed up or simply imposed from without. As has been said of the destruction of the cod fishery, it is not enough to blame outsiders, Newfoundlanders must look in the mirror. [31] The reflection, whether historical or current, may not always appear flattering, but there is no way to move forward without coming to terms with it.

NOTES ON INTRODUCTION

[1] *Encyclopedia of Newfoundland and Labrador*, Vol. 1 (St. John's: Newfoundland Book Publishers, 1981), pp. 722-723.

[2] *Newfoundland Quarterly*, Spring 1933.

[3] House of Commons (London), *Parliamentary Debates*, Vol. 284 (7 December, 1933), Col. 1847.

[4] *Newfoundland Royal Commission, 1933, Report* (London: H.M. Stationery Office, 1933), p. 1. Hereinafter referred to as *Amulree*.

[5] Proceedings of the House of Assembly, 1933, typescript (28 November, 1933). The debates of this session, as with the Spring 1933 session, were never published, but are contained in loose form at the Provincial Archives of Newfoundland and Labrador (PANL), St. John's. Select and edited excerpts appear in P. Neary, *The Political Economy of Newfoundland* (Toronto: Copp Clark, 1973).

[6] Ibid.

[7] F. C. Alderdice. *Manifesto* (St. John's: The Evening Telegram Ltd., 1932).

[8] This is in contrast to the standard accounts of the 1932 election which suggest commission government was the main issue promoted by Alderdice. See for example, P. Neary, *Newfoundland in the North Atlantic World. 1929-1949* (Kingston and Montreal: McGill-Queen's University Press, 1988), p.14; S. J. R Noel, *Politics in Newfoundland* (Toronto: University of Toronto Press, 1971), p. 203; *Encyclopedia*, Volume 1, p.717.

9 Edward Roberts, "Joseph Smallwood: Twenty-five Years On" in *Newfoundland Quarterly*, Winter/Spring 1998.

10 This is the general message in Ian McDonald (edited by J.K. Hiller), *"To Each His Own"—William Coaker and the Fishermen's Protective Union in Newfoundland Politics, 1908-1925* (St. John's: ISER, 1987).

11 The full text of Coaker's response to the Amulree report, as published in a letter to the *Evening Telegram*, 23 November 1933, is in Appendix E.

12 Ibid.

13 *Amulree*, p. 195.

14 Ibid., p. 2.

15 A complete exegesis of the historical evolution of Newfoundland's international "personality" is presented in W. C. Gilmore, *Newfoundland and Dominion Status: The External Affairs Competence and International Law Status of Newfoundland, 1855-1934* (Toronto: Carswell, 1988).

16 Magrath, Charles A., Papers, MG 30 E82, Vol. 12-18, National Archives of Canada; the microfilm at PANL is not complete and is a poor quality reproduction, MG 300, Reels 1-3.

17 J. K. Hiller and M. F. Harrington (eds). *The Newfoundland National Convention 1946-1948*, Vol. 1 (Kingston and Montreal: McGill-Queen's University Press), p. viii.

18 That the debates from this seminal event remain in disarray is an unfortunate reflection on inadequate levels of official support for what are otherwise commonly regarded as treasured archival resources.

[19] Hiller and Harrington. *The Newfoundland National Convention*, Vol. 1, p.xxii.

[20] W. C. Gilmore. "Law, Constitutional Convention, and the Union of Newfoundland and Canada," *Acadiensis*, 18, No. 2 (1989).

NOTES ON CHAPTER ONE

[1] The convention was held on the last weekend of November, although its proceedings are dated 25 December in the report published in W. F. Coaker, ed. *Twenty Years of the Fishermen's Protective Union of Newfoundland* (St. John's: Advocate Publishing Company Ltd., 1930; reprinted Creative Printers and Publishers Ltd., 1984), p. 236. See *Fishermen's Advocate*, 4 and 11 December, 1925.

[2] Noel. *Politics*, p. 179.

[3] See Appendix A for an excerpt from the speech.

[4] Magrath Papers, Testimony of Witnesses, 24 March, 1933. Like that of a number of other witnesses, Monroe's testimony was not recorded verbatim, but summarized in a report by the Commission secretary.

[5] *Amulree*, p.196.

[6] Ibid., p.192.

[7] Ibid., pp.81-82.

[8] W. J. Browne. *Eighty-four Years A Newfoundlander* (St. John's: Creative Printers and Publishers Ltd., 1981), p. 210.

[9] Noel. *Politics*, p. 218.

10 D. Alexander. "Newfoundland's Traditional Economy and Development to 1934" in J. K. Hiller and P. Neary, eds. *Newfoundland in the Nineteenth and Twentieth Centuries* (Toronto: University of Toronto Press, 1980), pp. 34-35. For a longer historical view of Newfoundland's development in relation to the North American economy, see H. Innis, *The Cod Fisheries: The History of an International Economy* (Toronto: University of Toronto Press, 1954).

11 D. Alexander. "Development and Dependence in Newfoundland, 1880-1970" in E. W. Sager, L. R. Fischer and S. O. Pierson, eds. *Atlantic Canada and Confederation* (Toronto: University of Toronto Press, 1983), p. 17.

12 A. F. Plumtre et al. "The Amulree Report (1933): A Review" in *Canadian Journal of Economics and Political Science*, No. 3, 1937.

13 *Amulree*, p. 37.

14 Ibid., p. 81.

15 D. W. Prowse. A *History of Newfoundland from the English, Colonial and Foreign Records* (London: Macmillan and Co., 1895; reprinted Belleville: Mika Studio, 1972), p.534.

16 For details of the riot, see ibid., pp. 488-491. For the later practice and effect of this principle, see G. O. Rothney, "The Denominational Basis of Representation in the Newfoundland Assembly, 1919-1962" in *Canadian Journal of Economics and Political Science*, No. 28, 1962.

17 *Amulree*, p. 185, p. 188; see also G. E. Gunn, *The Political History of Newfoundland 1832-1864*, (Toronto: University of Toronto Press, 1961).

18 Noel. *Politics*, p. 24.

19 J. Hiller. "Confederation Defeated: The Newfoundland Election of 1869" in Hiller and Neary, *Newfoundland*, p. 78.

20 Noel. *Politics*, p. 25.

21 *Amulree*, p. 24.

22 A. M. Fraser, "Relations With Canada", in R. A. Mackay, ed., *Newfoundland: Economic, Diplomatic, and Strategic Studies* (Toronto: Oxford University Press, 1946), p. 459.

23 *Amulree*, p. 29.

24 Noel, *Politics*, p. 28.

25 F. F. Thompson. *The French Shore Problem in Newfoundland: An Imperial Study* (Toronto: University of Toronto Press, 1961).

26 See McDonald, *To Each His Own*, pp.3-4.

27 David Macfarlane. *The Danger Tree* (Toronto: Macfarlane, Walter and Ross, 1995)

28 P. O' Brien. "The Newfoundland Patriotic Association: The Administration of the War Effort, 1914-1918", MA thesis, Memorial University, 1983, p.50.

29 McDonald. *To Each His Own*, Chapter 4.

30 M. Baker. "The Government of St. John's, Newfoundland, 1800-1921", PhD thesis, University of Western Ontario, 1980; M. Baker, "William Gosling and the Establishment of Commission Government", *Urban History Review*, No. 9 (1981).

31 B. Neis. "A Sociological Analysis of the Factors Responsibile for the Regional Distribution of the Fishermen's Protective Union of Newfoundland", MA thesis, Memorial University, 1980.

32 Coaker. *Twenty Years*, p. 5.

33 P. McInnis. "All Solid Along the Line: the Reid Newfoundland Strike of 1918", *Labour/Le Travail*, No. 26 (1990).

34 R. H. Cuff, "The Quill and the Hammer: The NIWA in St. John's, 1917-1925" in M. Baker et al., eds., *Workingman's St. John's: Aspects of Social History in the Early 1900s* (St. John's: Harry Cuff Publications Ltd., 1982).

35 Coaker, *Twenty Years*, p. 24. In response to a red-baiting campaign during the 1912 election, Coaker claimed to know nothing about the circulation among the union's members of the Canadian socialist paper, *Cotton's Weekly*. This denial was an attempt to cover the proselytizing efforts of the union's leading socialist, the school teacher, George Grimes. See D. Frank and N. Reilly, "The Emergence of the Socialist Movement in the Maritimes, 1899-1916" in R. J. Brym and R. J. Sacouman, eds., *Underdevelopment and Social Movements in Atlantic Canada* (Toronto: University of Toronto Press, 1979).

36 I. MacDonald. "W. F. Coaker and the Balance of Power Strategy: The Fishermen's Protective Union in Newfoundland Politics", in Hiller and Neary, *Newfoundland*; J. Feltham, "The Development of the F.P.U. in Newfoundland 1908-1923", MA theses, Memorial University, 1959, p. 136.

37 McDonald. *To Each His Own*, Chapter 6; Noel, *Politics*, pp. 142-148.

38 *Daily News*, 18 December, 1920 and 7 January, 1921.

39 *Evening Advocate*, 28 and 29 January, 1921.

40 Proceedings of the House of Assembly, 1921, p. 59. This session of the House was disrupted by demonstrations of unemployed workers. See E. Forbes, "Newfoundland Politics in 1921: A Canadian View" in *Acadiensis*, 4 (1975).

41 Coaker's alliance with Squires was marked with tension from the outset, owing to Squires' role in prolonging the conscription issue in 1917, with the deliberate intention of embarassing Coaker. McDonald, *To Each His Own*, p. 71.

42 Coaker, *Twenty Years*, p. 210.

43 J. Hiller. "The Politics of Newsprint" in *Acadiensis*, 19 (1990).

44 Noel. *Politics*, pp. 173.

45 Noel, *Politics*, pp. 167-170.

46 R.M. Elliot, "Newfoundland Politics in the 1920s: The Genesis and Significance of the Hollis Walker Inquiry" in Hiller and Neary, *Newfoundland*.

47 Coaker's support for Hickman may be explained in part by a personal relationship evident in the employment of Coaker's daughter Camilla at Hickman's firm. Coaker Papers, letter from A. E. Hickman, 12 May, 1921.

48 The previous designation for the merchant party was "Liberal-Labour-Progressive" (reflecting the alliance with St. John's labour) in the 1923 campaign against Squires. The 1924 "Liberal-Progressive" party was originally the anti-Liberal merchant coalition of 1919 that included Cashin, Crosbie and Hickman. *Encyclopedia* op. cit., pp. 710-714.

NOTES ON CHAPTER TWO

1 W. F. Coaker, *Circulars*, 20 September, 1924. Scammell was appointed as Coaker's successor as president in February, 1926. Coaker, *Twenty Years*, p. 251.

2 *Fishermen's Advocate*, 5 September, 1924.

3 *Encyclopedia*, Vol. 1, p.714. Bonavista had been the main centre of agitation of the United Fishermen's Movement, an outfit set up to oppose the FPU and Coaker. McDonald, *To Each His Own*, p. 120.

4 Coaker Papers, letter from A. E. Hickman, 8 October, 1924. *Advocate*, 31 October and 12 December, 1924.

5 Noel. *Politics*, p. 180.

6 Governor's Correspondence, GN 1/3/A 1925. "Memorandum from Committee of Council," 7 August.

7 Noel. *Politics*, p. 182.

8 Following the move to Port Union, the paper was claiming its circulation had increased by "thousands," making it "without doubt the most largely circulated paper in the country." *Advocate*, 8 May, 1925. Coaker said his goal was to increase circulation to its previous high of 8,000. Coaker, *Twenty Years*, p. 229.

9 *Evening Telegram*, 8 August, 1925.

10 *Advocate*, 14 August, 1925. The "alien imposter" is a reference to Morine, who was originally from Nova Scotia.

11 Ibid., 11 September, 1925.

12 Ibid., 22 October, 1925.

13 Coaker, *Twenty Years*, p. 368.

[14] Governor's Correspondence, 1925. Letter to L. S. Amery, 7 December, 1925.

[15] Ibid. Letter to Colonial Secretary, 23 October, 1925.

[16] Ibid. Letter to L. S. Amery, 7 December, 1925.

[17] Ibid. Letter From L.S. Amery, 12 February, 1926.

[18] Coaker, *Twenty Years*, p. 239.

[19] *Advocate*, 4 December, 1925.

[20] Ibid. Coaker said he was being asked who might serve on such a commision, indicating there was some prior discussion among his colleagues before he went public with the idea. He outlined a list of 18 potential candidates, including Bond, Squires and Cashin, suggesting they "would constitute the strongest Executive in the history of the country."

[21] Ibid.

[22] Ibid., 11 December, 1925. There was no notice given at the time to Coaker's speech by either the *Daily News* or the *Evening Telegram*, the country's two pro-government dailies.

[23] Ibid., 18 December, 1925.

[24] Ibid., 24 December, 1925.

[25] Ibid.

[26] Ibid., 8 January, 1926.

[27] Ibid., 18 December, 1925.

[28] Ibid.

29 In a note to readers Coaker stated the circulation of the Advocate was now "over five thousand," indicating an extremely high rate of return on the questionnaire and either an unusually engaged readership base, or much exaggeration in the paper's counting. In any event, the content of many of the published letters suggested a great deal of discussion in many communities. *Advocate*, 4 December, 1925.

30 Coaker Papers, letter from E. R. Chafe, 23 January, 1926.

31 Coaker, *Circulars*, 6 January, 1926.

32 Coaker Papers, letter from K. Brown, 8 December, 1925.

33 For the resignations, see Noel, *Politics*, p. 183.

34 Coaker Papers, letter from P. Cashin, 6 September, 1926. Cashin wrote to thank Coaker for the eulogy to his father (*Advocate*, 3 September, 1926) and to seek his assistance in purchasing a property for his mother in St. John's.

35 Ibid., letter from P. Cashin, 20 September, 1926.

36 Ibid., letter from P. Cashin, 4 January, 1927.

37 *Advocate*, 26 November, 1926.

38 Ibid., 31 December, 1926.

39 Ibid., 21 January, 1927.

40 Ibid., 4 February, 1927.

41 Ibid., 4 and 11 March, 1927.

42 Ibid., 2 December, 1927.

43 Ibid., 9 December, 1927.

[44] Ibid., 17 March, 1928. Smallwood claims credit for these events, and describes the mutual mistrust and animosity between Squires and Coaker as the main obstacle to the return of Squires. J. R. Smallwood, *I Chose Canada* (Toronto: Macmillan of Canada, 1973), p. 166.

[45] House of Assembly Proceedings, 1928, pp. 10-15.

[46] *Advocate*, 12 October, 1928.

[47] Coaker was not an early supporter of women's suffrage, and was implicated in the betrayals and broken promises on this issue during the first Squires government. Coaker viewed the franchise for women as a positive thing only insofar as the British experience had shown women to be a "safeguard" against instability because they "had no use for the red flag," and would work for "moral uplifting," particularly in promoting abstinence from alcohol. Coaker, *Twenty Years*, p. 227. See also M. I. Duley, "The Radius of Her Influence for Good" in L. Kealey, ed., *Pursuing Equality: Historical Perspectives on Women in Newfoundland and Labrador* (St. John's: ISER, 1993).

[48] *Advocate*, 24 October, 1928.

[49] See *Amulree*, pp. 182-186.

NOTES ON CHAPTER THREE

[1] Coaker, *Circulars*, 15 February, 1929.

[2] *Advocate*, 5 April, 1929.

[3] Ibid., 14 June, 1929.

[4] Ibid., 27 December, 1929.

[5] *Evening Telegram*, 2 January, 1930.

6 *Daily News*, 2 January, 1930.

7 Coaker, *Twenty Years*, pp. 367-385.

8 *Advocate*, 26 December, 1930.

9 *Daily News*, 3 January, 1931.

10 For a detailed review of the fishery issues as Coaker saw them, see *Advocate*, 22 May, 1931.

11 Noel, *Politics*, pp. 188-191. *Amulree*, pp. 51-53.

12 *Advocate*, 31 July, and 14 August, 1931.

13 Ibid., 30 October and 6 November, 1931.

14 Ibid., 20 and 27 November, 1931. One columnist claimed "thousands of people the country over read with delight" the appeal for commission government, and described a "manifest enthusiasm" for the idea, particularly if Coaker were to be its leader.

15 Ibid., 4 December, 1931.

16 Noel, *Politics*, pp. 193-196.

17 *Advocate*, 12 and 19 February, 1932. For a detailed review of these and subsequent events, an indispensable account is in J. Overton "Riots, Raids and Relief, Police, Prisons and Parsimony: The Political Economy of Public Order in Newfoundland in the 1930s" in E. Leyton, W. O' Grady, J. Overton, *Violence and Public Anxiety* (St. John's: ISER, 1992).

18 This account, and that of the riot following, is based on a reading of the *Advocate* and the two St. John's dailies through February, March and April, 1932.

19 *Census of Newfoundland and Labrador* (St. John's: 1935).

20 Archival film collection, Provincial Archives of Newfoundland and Labrador.

21 These articles were assembled and published in W. F. Coaker, *Past, Present and Future* (Port Union: 1932). See articles 8 and 9.

22 Ibid., article 3.

NOTES ON CHAPTER FOUR

1 *Amulree*, pp. 52-53.

2 *Encyclopedia*, pp. 717-718.

3 Alderdice wrote in a letter to the *Daily News*, 4 May, 1932, that this promise was in response to a request from Coaker.

4 Ibid.

5 *Evening Telegram*, 10 June, 1932.

6 *Advocate*, 27 May, 1932.

7 Ibid., 3 June, 1932. The paper did not endorse the Liberals, although it did offer a defense of Squires for having faced the country's financial problems "manfully." It referred to Coaker's appeal for a national administration to implement the commission proposal, noting that "hundreds" of men who had written and called the paper for advice seemed "lost."

8 Coaker, *Past, Present and Future*, articles 12 and 13. Overton, "Riots, Raids and Relief", pp. 254-266.

9 Neary, *Newfoundland*, pp. 14-15. Noel, *Politics*, p. 310.

10 *Advocate*, 17 February, 1933.

[11] Ibid., 2 April, 1933; *Daily News* and *Evening Telgram*, 30 March, 1933.

[12] *Daily News*, 28 March, 1933.

[13] Ibid., 24 February, 1933.The earlier debate was sponsored only by the MCLI and was either intended or seen afterwards as a dry run for a more substantial program.

[14] Ibid. At least three different witnesses used the same expression during the hearings. It was invoked again by the *News*, when the Amulree report was released, and attributed as an "historical pronouncement of the late E. M. Jackman during the last century" in an argument that responsible government was not suited to a large country with a small population. Ibid., 30 November, 1933.

[15] *Telegram*, 30 March and 4 April, 1933. Perlin's identity as the author of the column is noted in the "Confidential Diary" of H. F. Gurney, the British Trade Commissioner who visited Newfoundland in the spring and fall of 1933. Dominions Office Records, 35/386, 11 April, 1933.

[16] Magrath Papers, Testimony of Witnesses, 30 March, 1933. The record of interviews in these papers contains an opening list of intervenors and the dates they appeared.

[17] The Commission spent its first three weeks in St. John's, before leaving to visit nine other communities by train, and then Halifax and Montreal, before returning at the end of May for three weeks in the city and one final hearing in Bay Bulls.

[18] Magrath Papers, Testimony of Witnesses, 20 March.

[19] Ibid., 24 March.

[20] Ibid. 27 March. This is one occasion in the transcripts where the speakers from the Commission are identified.

More often, there is no such indication.

[21] Ibid., 23 March.

[22] Ibid., 24 March.

[23] Ibid.

[24] Ibid., 27 March.

[25] Ibid.

[26] Ibid., 31 March.

[27] Ibid.

[28] Ibid., 1 April.

[29] Magrath missed these hearings and did not rejoin until the Commission's return to St. John's in June.

[30] Magrath Papers, 17 April.

[31] These included five mill workers at Grand Falls, together representing three unions, three mill workers at Corner Brook, and one person each representing the Coopers' Union and the Longshoremen's Union at St. John's.

[32] Magrath Papers, 8 June.

[33] Ibid., 12 June.

[34] Ibid., 22 April.

[35] Ibid., 26 April.

[36] See discussion of British intentions in Chapter Five.

[37] Magrath Papers, 10 April. The other two women were representatives of the Newfoundland Outport Nursing and Industrial Association (NONIA).

[38] For a review of the complex interplay between conditions of destitution, political mobilization by the poor and

unemployed, and the response of authorities, see J. Overton, "Riots, Raids and Relief," op. cit.

[39] For instance, in Outerbridge's second interview, where he advocated disenfranchising "paupers," Magrath Papers, 9 June.

[40] Ibid., 2 June.

[41] Magrath Papers, Correspondence from the Public. The excerpts of letters which follow are from a file of correspondence which is not organized chronologically or otherwise, and are thus not annotated.

[42] Magrath Papers, Testimony of Witnesses, 8 June.

[43] Ibid., 31 May.

[44] Coaker received a telegram from Clutterbuck on 24 June requesting that he meet with the Commission. The next day he received another, saying the Commission was "grateful" for his offer, presumably to forward a written submission. In August he received a telegram acknowledging receipt of a memorandum. Coaker Papers. There were other submissions evidently received for which there is no record, including one from Richard Squires.

NOTES ON CHAPTER FIVE

[1] For example, *Evening Telegram*, 6 April, 1933.

[2] *Daily News*, 5 May, 1933.

[3] *Advocate*, 14 July, 1933.

[4] *Evening Telegram*, 11, 14, 15 and 18 July.

[5] *Advocate*, 4 August, 1933.

6 *Evening Telegram*, 5 August, 1933.

7 P. Neary, "'With great regret and after the most anxious consideration': Newfoundland's 1932 Plan to Reschedule Interest Payments", *Newfoundland Studies*, Vol. 10, Number 2 (1994).

8 Dominions Office Records, DO 414/58. "Memorandum by Royal Commission, 17th July, 1933"; "Note of Meeting Held at Treasury On 18th July, 1933."

9 Ibid.; "Letter from Lord Amulree to J. H. Thomas, 3 April, 1933."

10 Magrath Papers, Miscellaneous Correspondence, letter from C. A. Magrath to P. A. Clutterbuck, 16 September, 1933.

11 Ibid., letter from C. A. Magrath to Lord Amulree, 3 October, 1933.

12 For a detailed account of these events, see P. Neary, Newfoundland, pp. 24-39.

13 *Advocate*, 29 September and 2 October, 1933.

14 *Evening Telegram*, 16 September, 1933.

15 *Advocate*, 22 September, 1933.

16 H. F. Gurney, op. cit., 25 October, 1933.

17 Perlin wrote on the day of the report's release that he did not believe responsible government would be abolished, but that the existing parliament might be extended to prevent any interruption in implementing the recommendations.

18 *Evening Telegram*, 22 and 24 November, 1933. *Daily News*, 22 and 24 November, 1933.

[19] *Amulree*, pp. 197-198.

[20] Ibid., pp. 78-81.

[21] Ibid., pp. 54-57.

[22] Ibid., pp. 81-85.

[23] Ibid., p. 87.

[24] Ibid., pp. 88-89.

[25] Ibid., pp. 192-195.

[26] Ibid., p. 195.

[27] Ibid., p. 196.

[28] At a "largely attended" meeting of the Board of Trade to discuss the report, Cashin said he was not opposed to the recommendations, but thought they should be put to a referendum. There was one recorded vote against a resolution endorsing the report as presented—it was not his. *Evening Telegram* and *Daily News*, 25 November, 1933.

[29] House of Assembly Proceedings, 1933, typescript, 28 November.

[30] *Advocate*, 24 November, 1933.

[31] The amendments are contained in Neary, *Political Economy*, p. 53, and appear to be borrowed directly from Coaker's letter to the *Evening Telegram*. J. R. Smallwood claims to have been the source of Bradley's ideas, a notion challenged by J. K. Hiller, "The Career of F. Gordon Bradley," *Newfoundland Studies*, Volume 4, Number 2 (1988).

[32] Proceedings, 28 November, 1933.

[33] *Daily News*, 29 November, 1933. Both the *News* and the *Telegram* published detailed daily accounts of the proceedings.

[34] Proceedings, 1 December, 1933.

[35] *Advocate*, 22 December, 1933.

[36] *Parliamentary Debates*, 19 December, 1933, pp. 224-231. See also Neary, *Political Economy*, for excerpts.

[37] *Parliamentary Debates*, 14 December, p. 580.

[38] Ibid., p. 676.

[39] Ibid., 18 December, p. 940.

[40] Ibid., p. 952.

[41] Ibid., p. 962.

[42] *Advocate*, 29 December, 1933.

[43] Ibid., 15 December, 1933.

[44] *Advocate*, 1 December, 1933. Coaker believed it was the prospect of Squires leading the opposition to the report that persuaded the Commission from recommending a referendum. Ibid., 15 December, 1933. For Squires' telegram see Dominions Office Records, DO 414/58, "Telegram from Sir Richard Squires, 30 November, 1933."

[45] *Evening Telegram*, 27 November, 1933. *Daily News*, 29 November, 1933.

[46] Coaker, *Past, Present and Future*, Article 10.

NOTES ON CHAPTER SIX

[1] Overton, "Riots, Raids and Relief," p.278.

2 P. Neary, ed., *White Tie and Decorations: Sir John and Lady Hope Simpson in Newfoundland, 1934-1936* (Toronto: University of Toronto Press, 1996) p.152.

3 Ibid., p. 223.

4 Ibid., p. 104.

5 T. Lodge, *Dictatorship in Newfoundland* (London: 1937).

6 J. Webb, "The Responsible Government League and the Confederation Campaigns of 1948," *Newfoundland Studies*, Vol. 5, (1989).

7 J. R. Smallwood, *Coaker of Newfoundland: The Man Who Led the Deep-Sea Fishermen to Political Power* (Liverpool: C. Tinling and Co., Ltd., 1927). Smallwood wrote this book while in London in 1926. He sent a proposal to Coaker pleading for $300 to pay a publisher for a 3,000 copy press run, on the promise of the FPU taking 2,000 copies. It is not clear in this episode exactly who was the student of the art of self-promotion. Coaker Papers, letter from J. R. Smallwood, 30 December, 1926. The pamphlet, "A Sincere Appreciation of Newfoundland's Greatest Son," was published circa 1920 by the Advocate Publishing Company, St. John's.

8 Smallwood, *I Chose Canada*, p. 187.

9 J. Overton, "Economic Crisis and the End of Democracy: Politics in Newfoundland During the Great Depression", *Labour/Le Travail*, 26 (Fall 1990), p. 103.

10 Neary, *Newfoundland*, pp. 235-240.

11 Perlin's columns in this period were collected and published in F. C. Hollohan and M. Baker, eds., *A Clear Head in Tempestuous Times—Albert B. Perlin: The Wayfarer—Observations on the National Convention and the*

Confederation Issue 1946-1949, (St. John's: Harry Cuff Publications Ltd., 1986), p. 16.

12 Neary, *Newfoundland*, p. 234.

13 This interpretation, persuasively argued by Neary, is borne out in the minutae of records assembled and published in the three part, two-volume set, P. Bridle, ed., *Documents on Relations Between Canada and Newfoundland* (Ottawa: Department of External Affairs, 1974 and 1984).

14 *Amulree*, p. 197. Dominions Office Records, DO 414/58. "Despatch from Newfoundland Government, 2 December, 1933; "Telegram to the Newfoundland Government," 11 December 1933.

15 See for example, Harrington's essay in *The Newfoundland National Convention*, op. cit.

16 Ibid., p. 31 -32.

17 Ibid., pp. 345-346.

18 R. Gwyn, *Smallwood: The Unlikely Revolutionary* (Toronto: McClelland and Stewart Ltd., 1968), p. 84.

19 Webb, "The Responsible Government League" op. cit.

20 *The Newfoundland National Convention*, op. cit., p. 54.

21 Ibid., pp. 37-38.

22 H. Horwood, *Joey: The Life and Political Times of Joey Smallwood* (Toronto: Stoddart Publishing Co. Limited, 1989), p. 103.

23 *Newfoundland's National Convention*, p. 1369.

24 Ibid., p. 95.

25 J. R. Smallwood, *The New Newfoundland: An Account of the Revolutionary Developments Which Are Transforming*

Britain's Oldest Colony from "The Cinderella of the Empire" into One of the Great Small Nations of the World (New York: The Macmillan Company, 1931).

[26] See, for example, the results as examined in Neary, *Newfoundland*, pp. 320-24.

[27] *Encyclopedia*, Vol. 5, p. 287.

[28] Gwyn, *Smallwood*, pp. 125-126.

[29] P. Neary, "'A more than usual...interest:' Sir P.A. Clutterbuck's Newfoundland Impressions, 1950", *Newfoundland Studies*, Vol. 3, Number 2 (1987), p. 258.

[30] H. L. Ladd, "The Newfoundland Loggers' Strike of 1959" in W. J. C. Cherwinski and G. S. Kealey, *Lectures in Canadian Working Class History* (St. John's: Committee on Canadian Labour History, 1985).

[31] C. Martin, *No Fish and Our Lives: Some Survival Notes for Newfoundland* (St. John's: Creative Publishers, 1992), p. 209.

APPENDIX A

Excerpt from Address to the 17th Annual Convention of the FPU, November, 1925:[1]

The future depends more upon the right type of men elected than the policy they advocate. I may not be included in the next list of candidates appealing to the electorate. I have fought for certain ideals since 1909. These ideals were supported by a portion of the electorate and opposed by the other portion. I still believe in these ideals, but I see very little hope of putting them into effect and I would not again willingly undertake to carry political burdens and their incessant worries unless absolutely assured that the political ideals I have entertained for a lifetime would form a part of the political creed of a new government. I see many breakers ahead, and mountainous seas which will engulf the ship of State unless commanded by the best crew procurable in the land. Many big and far-reaching problems await to be solved. The fishing industry, the fish exporting business, the fish standardization problems, the producing of an improved grade of fish, the establishment of a great paper and smelting industry at Gander Bay, the establishment of a fleet of steamers to prosecute the sealfishery and do the carrying trade of the country are problems awaiting solution, but which will never be solved satisfactorily under the peculiar conditions which for the last thirty years have guided the electorate in the choice of its rulers. The chief aim of some political leaders has been to attain power or defeat their opponents regardless of the bluff and insincerity practised to attain the end. What I would like to see is a party appealing to the electorate on the single issue of passing a law to place the government of the country in the hands of nine men for ten years, electing the nine men somewhat on the lines pursued for years of selecting the Executive, that is to ensure denominational representation. I would like to see Catholic districts selecting three members of the Government of nine, the West Coast and Conception Bay selecting three more and the North three more, filling vacancies as they occur in each section and permitting the nine elected Commissioners to elect their own Chairman, who would be Prime Minister. The Deputy heads would administer the Departments. All legislation to be published prior to enactment to enable the public to discuss such or memorialize the Government in connection therewith. Such a policy pursued for ten years would produce reforms, establish industries, procure retrenchment and place the fishing industry on a sound businesslike basis. It would cut out graft, reduce the Civil Service list to its proper proportion, dispense, for a period, with the animosities and bitterness of party strife and permit the country to concentrate upon vital matters that await solution without having before its eyes day by day, as now, the spectre of the voters turning them out of office, because graft was limited, or jobs and pickings were unobtainable, or what the owners of inferior fish would do with their vote and influence in the event of being graded inferior by the proper inspection. Personally, after very considerable experience, I am convinced that the future of the country can best be served and attained under a Commission somewhat on the lines I have outlined. There would be no limit to the number of Candidates nominated for each division and the elections would be under the Election Law as far as applicable. The Party favouring such an issue, if elected to power, would have to convene the Legislature immediately after it became the Government and enact the necessary legislation. If the Upper House refused to pass such legislation its refusal would be overcome by the law of 1917 which enables the House of Assembly to enact laws without the concurrence of the Upper House. Following such an enactment dissolution would follow and an election take place to select the nine commissioners in three sections of three for each. The Catholic people would select their own representatives, the Church of England and Methodist would do the same. St. John's, Trepassey, Placentia, St. Mary's, Harbor Main and Bell Island would elect the three Catholic representatives, because the population is Catholic by a heavy majority. Conception Bay, Burin, Fortune Bay, Burgeo and the West Coast would elect three. The districts from St. Barbe to Trinity would elect three, which being largely Protestants would permit Protestants to be elected and there would be no trouble experienced in selecting three Methodist and three Anglicans. After ten years the Commission would issue a proclamation to elect members for the House of Assembly and Party politics would again dominate the elections and return a Party Government. I have given much though to the future development and progress of the country and I repeat, I am convinced that unless some such arrangement is made there can be no escape from the breakers nor can there be stable business progress. More progress would be made under such a Commission in ten years than would be possible in fifty years of Party government.

[1] As published in Coaker, *Twenty Years*, pp. 235-236.

APPENDIX B

Letter to Amulree Commission from Max E. Small[1]

26 March, 1933
Moreton's Harbour

Dear Sirs:

I noticed in your address given to the Assembly in the Newfoundland Hotel on March 16th, the account of which we read in the press seven days later, living as we do two hundred and fifty miles from St. John's, and thirty miles from the railway, which latter distance is now salt water ice, as we live on an island in Notre Dame Bay—we are almost cut off from happenings in our capital, but yet we try to follow with keenest interest what is given to us, true or otherwise of the workings of our country's government—that "you are anxious to get into the closest and most intimate contact with all sections of the country." So we have taken the liberty of approaching you on paper, and hoping that your lordship will pardon us if we intrude, and error in doing so.

I am a young man and it is not many years since the only interest I had in our government was to enjoy taking part in the usual election celebration of fireworks. But today nearly every young man and woman realizes that our country is in a terrible state of indebtedness, and that a way out must be found for her.

Usually, when a person is sick, they tell the doctor what they did before they got into the state that required them to call in the physician. You and your committee are the latter, appointed to suggest the remedy. Please bear with me while I state what, from my point of view and experience, I think caused our trouble.

As a kid I heard the late Sir Robert Bond give a lecture, I suppose it must be nearly twenty years ago, and everything that he said is gone from my memory except one of his phrases. He said "not only are we not in debt, but we have a quarter of million of a nest egg for a rainy day." No doubt but what I thought that was an enormous sum at the time, and that's why it stuck, coupled with the nest egg. If this was true (and I think it was) of the way in which Sir R. Bond ran the ship of state, it must have been the men who took charge of her later who has gotten her into her present difficulty.

Of these men we do not know anything personal, but we will tell you of some of the results of what they did; one who is now living in Bermuda[2] in luxury, with his special motor car and valet who sent agents all around this country collecting thousands of dollars, sometimes to the last one, so great was the faith in this man who was going to take the great burden off the fisherman. Blood money it was, in lots of incidents, won and wrung from the briny deep at great personal risks, laborious toil and losts. Money that was intended to buy food for the widow when the breadwinner had passed on; dollars saved for the eventide of life was dug out of stockings and cracked tea pots to reap in some of the 10% promised for its usury.

One agent collected $18,000 right here in this vicinity and a good bit of it in gold. Today old men and women are badly in need of this same money of which they can get neither the interest or principal. Then he was elected to the people's assembly to give him powers. How were they used? They were not—they were abused, the result being the FPU went up in smoke with a big bang and the ones that got hurt the most were the fishermen.

Next comes on the scene the master politician (the man who "couldn't remember" in the Hollis Walker inquiry) and tens of thousands of dollars of the taxes of our wage earners was given around to his friends, both in and outside the government. Why? Some of the papers said to keep them quiet, we don't know the truth. All we know is that Dr. Campbell, Dr. Barnes and dozens of others, who's published names in the press all got very large sums of money for which they made practically no returns to this country. The money was literally thrown away and wasted on roads that led to nowhere or into a swamp; on wells that were useless; on rams for bulls, or breakwaters, just to please the healer and not for the benefit of Newfoundland at all. The man played poor Newfoundland with one hand while with the other he played to his selfish interests, while the uneducated and simple underdog groaned and sweated with the bucksaw, or with frenzy pulled trawls and traps to pay from fifty to seventy five cents duty on the dollar of his spending money to help this man and his family have a sporty time at the Ritz-Carlton in London, or hop over to Paris or New York with expenses running as high or higher than fifty dollars a day.

Alas! the numerous picnics that have been enjoyed by our politicians at the expense of our people. If any other English speaking country had been bled and betrayed and exploited such as this one has been during the last fifteen or twenty years, there would have been a bigger uprising than that one which took place in St. John's last spring.

Again, our people were as honest as any people that you could meet, but they have learned a lot these last few years. They have seen how law has been lax when it touched the leaders, the powers that be, and that the very ones that had to administer the law always found a loophole through which they could escape its punishment, so that it has tended to breed a feeling of contempt, and has corrupted the fine honest minds of our people.

And the finishing stroke to our noble spirit of our inherited independence came when the "Free Dole" was introduced. We know that returns are supposed to be made in the form of labour, to build and repair roads, bridges and any other public works that need to be done. But as long as the system has to pass through the hands of the merchants and a committee of one or two of their friends corruption will be its biggest feature.

He would be a very poor business man who would advance from fifty to one hundred dollars worth of food to a family man in November, trusting to be paid for same the following July or August, with cod fish that is now swimming in the ocean, when he (the merchant) can get a Government to pay for it with cash. Also, influence counts when it comes to the sharing out of the dole orders by the relieving officers (not referring to one more than another).

It is useless to think that the big merchant is not encouraging this system. They are, and they are making good business out of it, as the results show. Yet we are a hundred million dollars in debt and they are still trying to add to it. What a pass we are got to! What a calamity!

We will never be in a better state of affairs till politics, as they have been served out to us in the past twenty years or more, are driven out of our land. A few years ago we had forty, I think it was, elected members. It was laughable, the trappings of an elephant on the back of a mouse was what we were supporting, and at the present time it is far too large and should be cut down to not more than five or, at the most, not more than seven honest, Christian and independent men, who would have no money invested in the country and no axes to grind, and paid a good salary so that they would be free from all influences, except the good of the state.

I believe these men can be found, or at least part of their number, in Newfoundland, and if these men were under the guidance of two or three of the very fine statesmen that the Mother Country has produced, and could lend for say five or six years until they were schooled into the art of sound government, and were able to take charge themselves, that we would see the dawning of a new day for this little island of ours.

Do not give us Confederation with Canada. Her own people are groaning as loud, if not louder than our own, from troubles that they are blaming to the results of the way they are governed. Canadian and U.S. citizens are being turned out of their homes because they cannot pay their taxes, but that can never happen to us as we are now. We are like the sea gull and the seal that are in plenty around our shores. We want to be free in the air, on the land and on the sea, to perch and bask where and when we will without anyone to say us nay. And if anyone is to be restricted it should be these who were in authority and who knowingly helped to bring this awful burden of debt on our land, to be borne by generations yet unborn.

I only voice the feelings and sentiments of thousands of our rising generations when I suggest that the men who did not do their best to prevent, but who were most instrumental in bringing on us this burden, should be forced to help pay it off with every copper they ever produce again. Yea!, a thousand, Yea! And bondholders should be cut down to three per cent.

I respectfully submit the foregoing lengthy and rambling remarks, blunderingly made no doubt to one of your education, but my chances to secure a good education have been very small.

May I receive your autograph on the enclosed postal card to know that you received this.

I remain,
yours respectfully,
(signed) Max Small

P. S. Of course it is needless for me to say that this has to be very confidential.

1 Magrath Papers, Correspondence From Public

2 This reference is to Coaker, whose estate was in Jamaica.

APPENDIX C

Excerpts from the Report
of the Amulree Royal Commission

Paragraphs 219 and 220

As a general statement, it is not too much to say that the present generation of Newfoundlanders have never known enlightened government. The process of deterioration, once started, could not be controlled. The simple-minded electorate were visited every few years by rival politicians, who, in the desire to secure election, were accustomed to making the wildest promises involving increased government expenditure in the constituency and the satisfaction of all the cherished desires of the inhabitants. The latter, as was not unnatural, chose the candidate who promised them most. This might be said of other countries, but in Newfoundland this cajoling of the electorate was carried to such lengths that, until the recent crisis brought them to their senses, the electors in many cases preferred to vote for a candidate who was known to possess an aptitude for promoting his own interest at the public expense rather than for a man who disdained to adopt such a course. They argued that, if a man had proved himself capable of using his political opportunities to his personal advantage, he would be the better equipped to promote the advantage of his constituents: an honest man would only preach to them.

The country was thus exposed to the evils of paternalism in its most extreme form. The people, instead of being trained to independence and self-reliance, became increasingly dependent on those who were placed in authority;

instead of being trained to think in terms of the national interest, they were encouraged to think only of the interests of their own district. Even within a district, or a church denomination, there was no public spirit; in the struggle to secure a decent living, the average man sought only his own advantage. The government was looked upon as the universal provider, and it was thought to be the duty of the Member for the constituency to see that there was an ever-increasing flow of public money. Since, outside St. John's, there was no municipal Government in the Island, and no direct taxation (apart from income tax, which was only payable by the few) the people did not pause to consider how the money was to be provided or what would be the end of this orgy of extravagance. They were content that their immediate wants should be satisfied. The politician was caught in his own meshes. As there was no local Government, he was expected to fulfill the functions of a Mayor and of every department of public authority. In addition, he was the guardian of local interests, the counselor and friend of every voter in the constituency and their mouthpiece in the Legislature of the country. Finally, under the peculiar system of administration adopted in Newfoundland, he was not only the liaison between the people and the Government but the channel through which the money voted by the Legislature for public purposes within his constituency was allocated and spent. The demands made upon him by the people increased from year to year. If a man lost his cow, he expected the Member to see that the Government provided him with another; if he had some domestic trouble, it was for the Member to put things right; if he fell ill, he looked to the Member to arrange for his removal to the hospital at St. John's at the public expense, to visit him in hospital where he obtained free treatment, and generally to see to his comfort at no cost to himself. If the wharf in a settlement fell into disrepair, the Member was expected to see that funds were provided by the Government to compensate the inhabitants for repairing it: notwithstanding that the material was to hand, that the lack of suitable wharfage was a serious inconvenience to the community, and that the necessary repairs could be effected in a few hours by willing workers, men would stand idly by and would prefer that the wharf should collapse into the sea rather than that they should repair it for their own benefit without public remuneration. The people were in fact taught to look to the Government for everything and to do as little as possible to provide for their own requirements. If the fishing was good, agriculture was neglected. If the fishing was bad, more attention was paid to the land, but the Government were expected to provide the seeds for the people to plant. Roads, bridges, town halls and public buildings; all these, often superfluous luxuries, the Government, through the Member, was expected to provide and maintain. The Member on his part, knew that unless he gave satisfaction to the people, he stood little chance of re-election: consequently, he was tempted to concentrate his energy on obtaining the maximum amount of money from the Government for allocation in his constituency. When it is said that, under the system adopted, there was no adequate audit of the money so allotted, it will be appreciated what opportunities there were for waste and extravagance. With no training in citizenship, and unversed in the elementary canons of public finance, the people were unable to realise that excessive expenditure would inevitably recoil on their own heads; the Government evidently possessed or could raise the money and, if that was so, it was held to be their right to have the maximum share of it.

Paragraphs 228-232

It should be appreciated, in the first place, that there is now no real distinction of principle between the political parties of Newfoundland. The names of Liberal, Conservative or Tory and Labour are in use but the division is rather one of persons. Secondly, the population of the Island is so small, and its financial resources are so restricted, that the choice of political candidates is severely limited. There is no leisured class, and the great majority of the people are quite unfitted to play a part in public life. As a rule, the Parliamentary Session only lasts about two months, and it might have been thought that the necessity for attendance during this short period would not have been an insuperable handicap to members of the commercial community. In fact, however, very few of the business men are prepared to enter politics, even though members of the Government are permitted to carry on their business while in office. This is not due to the lack of public spirit, but to the personal abuse to which candidates are subjected and to the feeling that, if elected, they would be suspected of being associated with corrupt dealings. A certain number of the legal profession have been ready to embark on a political career, but the professional classes generally have not responded. "Politics" have come to be regarded as an unclean thing which no self-respecting man should touch; the very word "politician" is virtually a term of abuse which carries with it a suggestion of crookedness and sharp practice. Many of the working people have a contempt for the politician. The so-called "modernisation" of politics, and the introduction into political life of men who sought to make a living out of their political activities, have been responsible for this deplorable state of affairs. At the last election, in 1932, the national danger was such that men offered themselves as candidates to whom the prospect was otherwise abhorrent. In normal circumstances, we are given to understand, it would not be possible for either party to count on the services of a greater number of candidates than would be required to fight each seat; and even this could only be achieved by lavish promises of election funds and subsequent rewards.

The spoils system has for years been in full force in Newfoundland. Given the conception that it is quite fair, whilst one's party is in power, to make what one can for oneself and one's friends, it is natural that in the minds of many people politics should be regarded simply as job farming. It has been the practice for each incoming Government to side-track or sweep away all Government employees who were either appointed by or were suspected of any connection, direct or indirect, with their predecessors, and to replace them with their own nominees, irrespective of the qualifications of the latter for the particular appointments assigned to them. St. John's is a small city of some 40,000 inhabitants. The educated class, from which the administrative grade of the Civil Service is recruited, is very small: the members of it are all known, if not related, to each other: everyone knows everyone else's business and it is a simple matter to ascertain which way any particular Civil Servant voted, or if he did not vote, what are the political leanings of his family and his relations. If he or they voted the wrong way, then, under the rules of the game, he must be deemed to have forfeited his appointment and must make way for a personal friend or supporter of the incoming Minister; although, in some cases, owing to lack of suitable personnel, Civil Servants have been permitted to continue in Government employment notwithstanding their alleged political affiliations.

In the case of the executive staff, post-election changes are commonly of a sweeping character with effects which manifest themselves in every corner of the Island. In such cases, the main consideration is the good will of the Member for the district concerned. Post Office and Railway employees, Customs Officials, Relieving Officers, Fishery and Timber Inspectors, and Wardens, members of the Fire Control staff, Lighthouse Keepers, and even Stipendiary Magistrates; all are liable to sudden dismissal, however competent their work, as the result of a change of Government.

The effect of this system on the administration of the country can well be imagined. The Civil Service, with no security of tenure, is left at the mercy of the politician. Constant changes have led to a lower standard of efficiency. Departments function as individuals rather than as a team; there is no cohesion, no continuity of policy and no incentive to take responsibility. Bitter experience has indeed shown that it does not pay to deal with any case, however petty, on its merits, without submission to the Minister concerned; the Service has been reduced to a state of abject subservience, apathy and indifference. In such circumstances it is obvious that it cannot attract the best candidates. The young men now leaving the secondary schools would make admirable material for recruitment to the Service, but few of them have any ambition other than to make their way in the United States or Canada; to enter the service of their country under conditions which, by placing good work at a discount, could only deprive them of their self-respect, cannot and does not appeal to them.

It is hardly surprising that, in these circumstances, the whole machinery of Government functions on political lines. Impartial administration is unknown and hardly expected. Breaches of the law or of current regulations are apt to be condoned if they are committed by the adherents of the party in power; the latter also expect special concessions, contracts and commissions, the waiving of customs duties and other inconvenient restrictions and numbers of petty favours, small in themselves but formidable in the aggregate. The adherents of the other party are deemed to have no ground for protest since their turn will come on a change of Government. These practices in themselves cannot but lead to an unhealthy tone in public life. Their effect is intensified by the interplay of religious denominational divisions and the ramifications of family relationships.

1 *Amulree*, op.cit., pp.82-83 and 86-88.

APPENDIX D

Notes on Commission Government [1]

Of the witnesses who have appeared before the Commission to date, 15 have been in favour of "Commission Government" for a period of years and 8 against. It will be seen from the attached list that those in favour are made up of 3 members and 1 ex-member of the present Cabinet, 1 ex-Prime Minister, one member of the Upper House, 1 Minister in the last Government, 2 Civil Servants, 1 Bank Manager, 2 Merchants, 1 lawyer and 2 commercial men. Those against comprise 4 members of the present Cabinet, the late Prime Minister and his Finance Minister, 1 merchant and 1 commercial man.

The advocates of Commission Government have in the main been actuated by the genuine belief that in no other way will it be possible to satisfy the essential needs of the country, namely to stamp out graft and corruption, get rid of the professional politician, and lead the people back to a sense of independence and self-reliance. They are united in the idea that it is 25 years of politics that has led to the breakdown of responsible government, and that, the crash having come, it would be suicidal to attempt to rebuild on the same foundation. It is only by firm control and a prolonged political holiday, they claim, that the country can be saved.

Those who oppose Commission Government do so for four reasons: (a) On account of the humiliation involved; Commission Government would mean Newfoundland is not fit to govern herself. (b) It might necessitate reversion to the status of a Colony and this would mean putting the clock back. (c) While the people might accept it today they would soon be dissatisfied and the position of the Commissioners would become intolerable. (d) The composition of the Commission would in any case present serious difficulties.

It will be observed from the attached list that the opponents of this form of government are mostly politicians. This is only natural since it is at the politicians that the proposal is aimed. On the other hand the Cabinet Ministers and the others in the opposite camp are not all so disinterested as might appear, since it is not unfair to say that some at least see in the proposal an attractive and patriotic device for keeping their own party in power and completing the ruin of their political opponents. These might have different views if the Commission were to be composed of outsiders.

Individual suggestions as to the form which Commission Government might take have naturally varied with the angle from which the problem has been approached. But for the purposes of this note it will be convenient to consider the suggestions under two heads: (A) Those which would not necessarily impair the status of the Island as a Dominion and (B) those which would do so.

A. *Commission Government in a form which would not necessarily impair the status of the Island as a Dominion.*

It may be taken as axiomatic that any proposal which involved the disappearance of the Legislature would be inconsistent with the existing constitutional instruments. The Constitution of Newfoundland is somewhat complicated, being partly written and partly unwritten, the former being contained partly in Letters Patent and Royal Instructions, partly in Acts of the U.K. Parliament and partly in Acts of the Newfoundland Legislature. The main instrument is the Letters Patent of the 28th March, 1876 which constitute the office of Governor and define the Governor's powers and authorities. Clause III. of the Letters Patent deals with the Constitution of the Legislative Council and Clause IV. empowers the Governor "to summon and call together the General Assembly…, and also, from time to time, in the lawful and accustomed manner, to prorogue the Legislative Council and the House of Assembly…, and from time to time to dissolve the said House of Assembly." Clause V. authorises and empowers the Governor, *with the advice and consent of the Legislative Council and Assembly*, to make laws for the public peace, welfare and good government of Newfoundland.

Detailed provisions regarding the House of Assembly are contained not in the Letters Patent but in Newfoundland Acts, but it is clear from the above Clauses that the Letters Patent postulate the existence of a Legislative Council and House of Assembly and further that the Governor has no power of legislation except with the advice and consent of the two Houses. Any proposal to enable the Governor to act independently of the Legislature, which would be dissolved for the time being, would therefore seem prima facie to require amendment of the Letters Patent.

On the other hand, it may be argued that the Letters Patent are only a part of Newfoundland's written constitution, and must be read subject to her unwritten constitution, namely to the advance in constitutional usage and practice which has taken place since 1876. At the time that the Letters Patent were issued and for many years afterwards Newfoundland was a Colony and, as such, subject in the last resort, to control from the United Kingdom. In the course of time her position became that of a self-governing Colony with Dominion status and the extent to which she became immune from interference is shown by the correspondence with Downing Street at the time of the Reid contract in 1897. Finally, with the passage of the Statute of Westminster in 1930, she ceased to be a Colony and became a Dominion. Yet throughout this period the Letters Patent have remained unamended. It is inevitable in the circumstances that certain clauses in the Letters Patent should be obsolete and others obsolescent, from which it might be argued that it is Newfoundland's status as a Dominion rather than the former constitutional instruments which must be the determining factor. If some clauses of the Letters Patent are obsolete, why not others? If this argument is sound, it might suffice for the Newfoundland Government to enact legislation dissolving the Legislature for a period of years and placing all executive and legislative power in the hands of the Governor and an Executive Council to be nominated by him. But while the position is not free from doubt—indeed it is a nice constitutional point—the correct answer is I think, that it is merely the *restrictive* Clauses of the Letters Patent that have become obsolete, i.e. those which imply control from the United Kingdom, and that the remainder, which carry no such implication, continue in full force as the foundation of the constitution of the Island which can only be altered by His Majesty under the powers specially reserved in the Letters Patent to the Sovereign. This conclusion is reinforced by reference to the Commission issued by the King to the present Governor (14th October, 1932) which authorises, empowers and commands His Excellency to "exercise and perform all and singular the powers and directions contained in" the Letters Patent. In these circumstances, it is, I think, to be assumed that any steps for the suppression of the Legislature would require amendment of the Letters Patent, a course which, as shown under B, would inevitably impair the status of Newfoundland as a Dominion.

Given, then, that the Legislative Council and House of Assembly must be retained in being, how could Commission Government be established? It would seem that this could only be carried out in one of two ways:

1. The Government to appoint a Commission, composed of such members as they might think fit, and to empower them to take executive charge of all Government Departments and all public business. The Commission would have no legislative authority but it would be understood that whenever it required fresh legislation to be passed it would make recommendations to the Government who would undertake, in the absence of strong reasons to the contrary, to accept them and to put the necessary legislation through Parliament. The Government would further undertake not to enact legislation except on the recommendation of the Commission. Under this scheme the Commission would be subordinate to the Executive Council (which would be retained in being on a purely honorary basis) but would be immune from interference by that body except and in so far as fresh legislation might be required. The weakness of the scheme lies in the fact that since most executive work depends in the last resort on financial provision and since financial provision requires legislative sanction, the freedom of action granted to the Commission might prove to be illusory.

2. The Government to pass an Act reconstituting the Executive Council (as they are fully entitled to do under Clause II. of the Letters Patent of 1876). They might for instance, decide that the Executive Council, instead of consisting of twelve members as at present, should in future consist of the Prime Minister and the Secretary of State, and four members to be nominated by the Governor (the understanding being that two would be selected from Canada and two from the United Kingdom). They could further provide by legislation that those members of the Executive Council who were not already members of the House of Assembly should be ex-officio members of the body. The Executive Council would then proceed , just as they do today, to take charge of the executive business of the Island and the members would between them be responsible for running the various Government departments, for framing policy and for carrying through the necessary reforms. The Executive Council would in fact be the "Commission", with the Prime Minister (subject to the Governor) at the head of it and the Prime Minister would depend on his majority in Parliament for putting through the fresh legislation on which the Commission might decide. This might work very well but the weakness of the scheme lies in the fact that all members of the existing Executive Council, other than the Prime Minister and the Secretary of State would be thrown out of office and while they would no doubt behave themselves at first they might before long constitute a disgruntled bloc in the House. The scheme could only work satisfactorily as long as the Prime Minister was absolutely sure of his majority.

B. *Commission Government in a form which would impair the status of Newfoundland as a Dominion.*

It is to be expected that neither of the forgoing

schemes would be satisfactory to the advocates of Commission Government since neither would interfere with the machinery of Parliament, still less provide for its suppression. It would thus be possible for a new Government to reverse the action taken by the present Government and to restore the status quo with all its dangers. If it should be desired to safeguard the country against this possibility, it would be necessary to suspend the present Parliamentary system and this would involve the alteration of the Letters Patent.

Assuming that the Government wished to go to these lengths, the appropriate procedure from the constitutional standpoint would be the submission of an Address to the Sovereign from both Houses of the Newfoundland Legislature setting out the grounds on which the provision of the Letters Patent was desired and praying for the issue of new Letters Patent under which both the executive and the legislative power would be vested in the Governor who would be assisted by an Executive Council consisting of x members to be nominated by him. It could be recommended that x/2 should be chosen from Newfoundland, x/2 from the United Kingdom, and x/2 from Canada, or such other proportions as the Government might see fit to suggest. Alternatively, if it were desired to do so, it might be recommended that all the members should be chosen from outside Newfoundland. Further recommendations might be that there should be an Advisory Council composed of prominent men in Newfoundland (who would serve in an advisory capacity) and that the new regime should be subject to review either at the end of a stated period or when Newfoundland was again able to pay her way. On the assumption that these recommendations were adopted by His Majesty, arrangements could then be made for the issue of new Letters Patent revoking the existing Letters Patent and containing provisions in the sense desired. The existing Royal Instructions would also have to be revoked and fresh instructions issued, and it would further be necessary for a new Commission to be issued to the Governor.

But while from the standpoint of procedure no special difficulty would seem to arise (though action of this kind is of course unprecedented) the implications of such a course would undoubtedly be far-reaching.

In the first place, it is clear that, both executive and legislative power having been invested in the Governor, His Excellency could not be left in the air as a virtual dictator. But, it may be said, Newfoundland is a Dominion, and, as such, able to dispose of her own destiny. Why then should she not have a dictator if she wished? If the South African Parliament for instance chose to abdicate its functions and place all executive and legislative power in the hands of the Governor General, would there be any cause for interference? Whatever the answer to this last question (which would be a nice exercise in constitutional theory) it is clear that Newfoundland would, in any case, be regarded as in a different position from that of any of the larger Dominions. It will not have escaped notice that the Governor is a Governor, and not a Governor-General. It may be taken as axiomatic that a small and backward community like this could not be left to the tender mercies of a Governor appointed from home without supervision of some sort. At the present time the Island enjoys full "responsible government," i.e., a system of government under which Ministers elected by the votes of the people are responsible to the people for the good government of the country, the Governor being a constitutional figurehead who is required (except possibly in certain contingencies into which it is not necessary to enter here) to act on his Minister's advice. If there ceased to be elected Ministers and the Governor and the Governor was given complete freedom of action (either alone or as "Governor-in-Council), it would be necessary for him to be accountable to some authority for his actions and (unless this form of government could be made to fit in with some wholly novel scheme of political union with Canada) this authority could only be the U.K. Govt. It follows that the introduction of "Commission Government" in this form would automatically deprive Newfoundland of Dominion status and would degrade her to that of a Colony under U.K. control. In other words the Governor would be responsible to the appropriate Secretary of State in London for the good government of the Island and the Secretary of State would be responsible to Parliament, who in turn would be responsible to the U.K. electorate.

It follows from this reasoning that the issue of new Letters Patent would not in itself be sufficient to secure the end desired. If the U.K. Parliament is to assume the responsibility, it would be necessary to obtain its consent. In view of the recently passed "Statute of Westminster," "Section 1 of which defines the expression "Dominion" as including Newfoundland, the appropriate procedure would doubtless be the passage of a further Act of Parliament (which would be specifically stated to have been passed with the request and to the consent of the Newfoundland Government) providing for the administration of Newfoundland, as a Colony.

The assumption by the U.K. Government of responsibility for the good government of Newfoundland would in turn involve responsibility for its finances. This would necessitate a grant-in-aid equivalent to the amount of the annual deficit. The novelty of the situation (vis., the demotion of a Dominion), the size of the deficit, and the notorious mis-management, not to say corruption of previous Newfoundland Governments, would all combine to attract attention and there would no doubt be many to say that the United Kingdom had already shouldered enough responsibilities. It would be idle to pursue speculation too far, but the conclusion naturally suggests itself that, if the U.K. taxpayer were to be saddled with this additional burden, the least that could be done to pacify him would be to link the Colony to sterling and to revise the tariff on a preferential basis.

A further point which ought not to be overlooked is that the position of the present Government would be affected. Under a regime of this kind, a Governor of the administrative type would be required (as Mr. Dunfield has already acted) and the present Governor, whose training and experience have lain in other directions, would no doubt feel himself unfitted for the post.

If such a form of Government were successfully introduced, could it last? If it were possible to include in the Executive Council (i.e. the "Commission") the leaders of both political parties, there might be a chance of it doing so, but this is unfortunately not the case. Given the exclusion of Sir R. Squires, the changeable and temperamental nature of the people, and the fact that the "Commission" would have to indulge in unpopular reforms, it is difficult not to share the belief of those who affirm that the position of the "Commissioners" would soon become intolerable. If the people were to be stampeded by ex-politicians, as they might quite easily be in default of a quick recovery, a garrison might even be needed. But apart altogether from such possibilities, agitation for a return to the status quo could only be a matter of time; the more drastic the change the more violent the reaction. In the face of popular sentiment not even a garrison would avail.

The foregoing considerations would apply to all the suggested forms of "Commission Government" which would involve the suppression of the Legislature. The danger of the country being stampeded by Sir R. Squires and his associates would of course apply also to those which would allow of the Legislature being retained in being. But it would seem from the above analysis that if some such form of Government should be considered essential for the immediate future, the safest form and that which could be introduced with the least embarrassment both to Newfoundland and the United Kingdom is that discussed under paragraph (2) of head (A). This would not involve the suppression of Parliament, and would be fully consistent with the constitutional instruments; and though it would theoretically be liable to reversal by a new Ministry the danger could, if necessary, be countered by an extension of the life of the present Parliament for such period as might be considered appropriate in the light of the then prevailing political conditions. But whether even this comparatively mild form of "Commission Government" could be introduced without a referendum is of course a matter which the Government alone would be competent to decide.

PRO	ANTI
Monroe (if first put to Cashin the country by party formed on that basis).	Cashin
Taylor—dictators from outside	Walsh
Stafford—outsiders	Horwood
Bowring—some form or other	McNamara
Baird—U.K. to take over Newfoundland for a few years.	H. Winter
Gushue—if Confederation not possible	Sir R. Squires
Sir M. Winter (but with Parliament still continuing)	W. J. Browne
Angel—schoolmaster government	L. Outerbridge
Ayre—Commission of 3 from outsideand Advisory Board (hon.) of 10 or 12.	
Emerson—7 or 8; 2 from U.K., 1 or 2 from Canada, remainder local.	

PRO	ANTI

Dunfield (Commission of 6
presided over by Governor
of
C.O. type, cf. Nigeria; Mr.
Alderdice & Lieut.
(Emerson),
Sir R. Squires & Lieut.
(Sir T. Cook) and two men
of
standing from U.K.)

Lake—as leading to
Confederation
(Commission of 5—3
local, 1 U.K.,
1 Canada).

Archibald—Bell Island—
absolute
control for the time being.

H. Mitchell—if referen-
dum first.

1   This document is from the Magrath Papers,
"Miscellaneous". It is signed by P.A. Clutterbuck, with a
note that it was presented 15 Sept. 1933.

APPENDIX E

Letter from William Coaker to *Evening Telegram*, 23 November 1933

Dear Sir—You request my views on the Report of the Royal Commission: but I feel sure you appreciate the difficulty, if not the impossibility, of forming a considered opinion or coming to any definite conclusion within a few days in reference to such a comprehensive, complex and important document, the preparation of which required the concentrated attention of its compilers extended over a period of several months.

However the whole appears to be summed up in the despatch dated the 19th., inst., from the Rt. Hon. the Secretary of State for the Dominions, to the Hon. the Prime Minister of Newfoundland in reply to the latter's request for an indication of the attitude of the British Government to the recommendations of the Commission. Perusing that Despatch, it is quite obvious that the immediate welfare of Newfoundland and Newfoundlanders is not its main theme. Its text is based on, (1) the political situation facing the country, and (2) the necessity of protecting the bond holders and financial creditors of Newfoundland; whereas our pressing and imperative needs are the feeding and clothing of our starving and destitute people during the coming winter; and the finding of remunerative employment in productive labour for over twenty thousand of our male population, in order to enable them to resume the support of themselves and their families before another year passes. These are the questions with which the country is concerned—of even paramount importance to outside interests, financial or otherwise; but these questions the Report fails to effectively answer.

What remedial suggestions have the Commissioners offered in so far as the development of our fisheries is concerned? They make no definite recommendation only, namely, the spending of $165,000 to provide four schooners to test out the possibilities of the fishing grounds and the establishment of six bait depots as an experimental step toward the provision of bait supplies: and the only help the Report contemplates giving to the rehabilitation of our main industry is the suggestion to create a new department of natural resources embracing the fisheries, forests, agriculture and mines, presided over by a Commissioner, not from Newfoundland, but from England. Is that assisting our staple industry as was expected? Does that afford Newfoundland the aid so urgently required to man her fishing fleets, finance their outfitting, and assure to those who prosecute the voyage, reasonable hope of obtaining suitable returns to maintain their families and themselves? It is true the Report contains many references to the necessity of restoring the fishing industry of the country, but it lamentably fails to solve our problems in that respect; and many of the proposals which the Report indicates in my opinion, if given effect, would only make matters worse. They may sound well in the theory, but in the main they are impracticable and offer no remedy for the ills from which this industry has been suffering for the past few years.

The main principle underlying the Report is the establishment of a Commission form of government for this country. I approve of Government by Commission—provided proper safeguards are afforded our people. My ideas as to the creation of this new system of government and its operation in the administration of the country's affairs differ materially however from those of the Commissioners. I am absolutely opposed to the scheme of government as outlined in the Report. Not alone does it involve the complete abrogation of our rights of self-government, but proposes to set up a governing body vested with the widest and most autocratic powers, uncontrolled and uncontrollable so far as the people of Newfoundland are concerned who are denied even the right of selection of those to whom they are asked to surrender their liberties. That would not be government! That would be sheer despotism and contrary to every principle upon which government within the British Empire is founded. It is humiliating enough to have to witness the giving up of responsible government, but to be plunged from the status, theoretical though it may have been, of a self-governing Dominion of the Crown to a position below that of the ordinary Crown Colony, is degrading. We should be put on a par with one of the subject races—an intolerable situation to even contemplate. A Commission selected by, and properly representative of, the people, to govern the country for a definite term of years, freed from the disturbances and disadvantages of party politics, might very well prove the salvation of Newfoundland; but there is a vast difference between that system of government and the plan proposed by the Royal Commission. Greatly as default by this country in its financial obligations is to be deplored, I think it is preferable to the acceptance of the proposals as contained in the Report.

Our Legislature has been called together for Monday next to deal with the report. I cannot for a moment bring myself to believe that there will be any hasty decision reached on what is perhaps the most momentous question ever submitted to the consideration of the people's representatives—involving not alone the political destinies of our country, but the intimate interests of every man, woman and child in Newfoundland. Obviously it is not a matter for any snap judgement, and realizing the interests at stake, appreciating the fact that not only is the protection of the creditors of Newfoundland concerned, but the most sacred rights and liberties as well, it must be presumed that the most mature thought will be given to the Report and the recommendations it contains, before any action is taken. Every precaution should be observed to see that every phase of the subject is exhaustively considered before any definite conclusion is reached. To rush a matter of such importance through the Legislature may very well involved a disaster to the people of this country, even more far reaching than that conjectured by the Commissioners.

In my opinion the Legislature would be unwise if it accepted the recommendations in their present form; but it would be false to its trust and its members recreant in their duty to the people they represent if they tolerated any attempt to rush the matter. It is not too much to say that those who hastily or inadvisably or for any unworthy motive vote for the acceptance of the Report in its present form, will be remembered in the history of this country as traitors to the land that bore them.

There are certain acceptable phrases in the Report, but there are many objectionable features. The latter may be removed if time is given to analyse and properly consider the recommendations and suggest some counter-proposals. An opportunity for this should be afforded, and it is only fair, not alone to the members of the Legislature, but to the public at large, that time should be given in order to properly assess the value and effect of the document upon which the destinies of this country depend. The suggestion which I venture to make is that, following the discussion on the Report, to take place on Monday next, the House should rise for an interval sufficiently long to enable the Report to be exhaustively studied, as well by the representatives of the people, as by the public itself; and in so far as objections to the recommendations may be disclosed, an opportunity should also be afforded for the submission of counter-proposals to the British Government; and to that end a Commission should be appointed to proceed if necessary, to England, to confer with the representatives of the British Government to see whether some more acceptable plan could be evolved, and some better method devised to safeguard our national obligations and assure the recovery of our country at the same time, protecting us against the ill-effects which are bound to follow if the proposals in their present form are carried out.

I do not think it is too much to ask that this country be allowed at least a few weeks to properly consider a Report which has taken months to prepare. In that the recommendations involve the surrender of our rights of self-Government, I seriously question the power of the Legislature to assent to the abrogation of these rights without first having the matter submitted to the people, and I feel confident that were any other country within the British Empire faced with a decision which we are now asked to make, nothing would be done by the representatives of the people unless and until the question was first submitted at least by way of a plebiscite to the determination of the people themselves.

Yours truly,
W.F. Coaker
St. John's, November 23rd.

BIBLIOGRAPHY

PRIMARY SOURCES

Alderdice, W. "Election Manifesto." Pamphlet published for the election campaign of 1932.

Census of Newfoundland and Labrador, St. John's, 1935.

Coaker, William. Private papers; Coaker Circulars, Collection of correspondence with FPU regional councils. Centre for Newfoundland Studies.

——.*Past, Present and Future*, Port Union, 1932.

——.*Twenty Years of the Fishermen's Protective Union*, Port Union, 1930.

Documents on Relations Between Canada and Newfoundland, Parts 1 and 2, Ottawa, 1974, 1984. P. Bridle, ed,

Dominion's Office Records, 1933, 414/58; 35/386.

Governor's Correspondence, 1925, GN 1/3/A, Provincial Archives of Newfoundandland and Labrador.

C. A. Magrath papers. National Archives of Canada. Microfilm, Provincial Archives of Newfoundland and Labrador.

The Newfoundland National Convention 1946-1948, J. K. Hiller and M. F. Harrington, eds., Montreal, 1995.

Newfoundland Royal Commission, 1933, Report, London.

Political Debates, House of Commons, London, 1933.

Proceedings of the Newfoundland House of Assembly, 1921-1931.

Proceedings of the Newfoundland House of Assembly, 1933, typescript, Provincial Archives of Newfoundland and Labrador.

Newspapers

Evening Advocate, 1921.

Fishermen's Advocate, 1924-1933.

The Evening Telegram, 1924-1933.

The Daily News, 1921, 1924-33.

SECONDARY SOURCES

Articles

Alexander, David. "Development and Dependence in Newfoundland, 1880-1970" in Eric W. Sager et al., eds., *Atlantic Canada and Confederation*. Toronto, 1983,

——."Newfoundland's Traditional Economy and Development to 1934" in James K. Hiller and Peter Neary, *Newfoundland in the Nineteenth and Twentieth Centuries: Essays in Interpretation*. Toronto, 1980.

Baker, Melvin. "William Gosling and the Establishment of Commission Government," *Urban History Review*, 9, 3 (1981).

Chisholm, Jessie. "Organizing on the Waterfront: the St. John's Longshoremen's Protective Union (LSPU), 1890-1914," *Labour/ Le Travail*, 26 (1990).

Cuff, Robert. "The Quill and the Hammer: The NIWA in St. John's, 1917-1925," in R. Cuff et al., eds., *Workingman's St. John's: Aspects of Social History in the Early 1900s*. St. John's, 1982.

Duley, Margot Iris. "The Radius of Her Influence for Good" in L. Kealey, *Pursuing Equality*, St. John's, 1993.

Frank, David and Nolan Reilly. "The Emergence of the Socialist Movement in the Maritimes, 1899-1916," in R. Brym and R. Sacouman, eds., *Underdevelopment and Social Movements in Atlantic Canada.* Toronto, 1979.

Elliot, R. M. "Newfoundland Politics in the 1920s: The Genesis and Significance of the Hollis Walker Enquiry" in J. K. Hiller and P. Neary, *Newfoundland in the Nineteenth and Twentieth Century: Essays in Interpretation.* Toronto, 1980.

Forbes, Ernie. "Newfoundland Politics in 1921: A Canadian View," *Acadiensis*, 4 (1975).

Gilmore, William. "Law, Constitutional Convention and the Union of Newfoundland & Canada" in *Acadiensis*, 18, No. 2 (1989).

Hiller, James K. "Twentieth Century Newfoundland Politics: Some Recent Literature," *Acadiensis*, 20 (1991).

——."The Politics of Newsprint: the Newfoundland Pulp and Paper Industry, 1915-1939," *Acadiensis*, 19 (1990).

——."F. Gordon Bradley," *Newfoundland Studies*, 4, 2 (1988).

——."Confederation Defeated: The Newfoundland Election of 1869" in James K. Hiller and Peter Neary, eds., *Newfoundland in the Nineteenth and Twentieth Centuries.* Toronto, 1980.

Innis, Harold. "Basic Problems of Government in Newfoundland," *Canadian Journal of Economics and Political Science*, 3 (1937).

Kealey, Gregory S. "1919: The Canadian Labour Revolt," *Labour/Le Travail*, 13 (1984).

Ladd, H. Landon. "The Newfoundland Loggers' Strike of 1959" in W. J. C Cherwinski and G. Kealey, eds., *Lectures in Canadian Labour and Working Class History*, St. John's, 1985.

McCann, Philip. "Denominational Education in the Twentieth Century in Newfoundland," in W. McKim, ed., *The Vexed Question: Denominational Education in a Secular Age*. St. John's, 1988.

McDonald, Ian. "W. F. Coaker and the Balance of Power Strategy: The Fishermen's Protective Union in Newfoundland Politics," in James K. Hiller and Peter Neary, eds., *Newfoundland in the Nineteenth and Twentieth Centuries: Essays in Interpretation*. Toronto, 1980.

McInnis, Peter. "All Solid Along the Line: The Reid Newfoundland Strike of 1918," *Labour/Le Travail*, 26 (1990).

Neary, Peter. "A more than usual interest: Sir P. A. Clutterbuck's Newfoundland Impressions, 1950" in *Newfoundland Studies*, 3, 2 (1987).

——. "With great regret and after the most anxious consideration. Newfoundland's 1932 plan to reschedule interest payments" in *Newfoundland Studies*, 10, 2 (1994)

Roberts, Ed. "Joey Smallwood" in *Newfoundland Quarterly*, Fall 1997.

Rothney, Gordon. "The Denominational Basis of Representation in the Newfoundland Assembly, 1919-1962," *Canadian Journal of Economics and Political Science*, 28, 4 (1962).

Overton, James. "Economic Crisis and the End of Democracy: Politics in Newfoundland During the Great Depression," *Labour/Le Travail*, 26 (1990).,

——."Public Relief and Social Unrest in Newfoundland in the 1930s: An Evaluation of the Ideas of Piven and Cloward" in Gregory S. Kealey, ed., *Class, Gender and Region: Essays in Canadian Historical Sociology*, St. John's, 1988.

——."Riots, Raids and Relief, Police, Prisons and Parsimony: The Political Economy of Public Order in Newfoundland in the 1930s" in E. Leyton, W. O' Grady and J. Overton, *Violence and Public Anxiety*, St. John's, 1992.

Webb, Jeff. "The Responsible Government League and the Confederation Campaigns of 1948" in *Newfoundland Studies*, 5, 1989.

BOOKS

Basset, R. *Nineteen Thirty One*, London, 1958.

Chadwick, J. *Newfoundland: Island into Province*, Cambridge, 1967.

Encyclopedia of Newfoundland and Labrador, Vol.1, 1982; Vol. 5, 1984. Newfoundland Book Publishers.

Gilmore, William. *Newfoundland and Dominion Status*, Toronto, 1988.

Gunn, Gertrude. *The Political History of Newfoundland, 1832–1864* Toronto, 1967.

Gwynn, Richard. *Smallwood: The Unlikely Revolutionary*, Toronto, 1974.

Hiller, James and Peter Neary, eds. *Twentieth Century Newfoundland: Explorations*, St. John's 1993.

Hobsbawm, Eric. *The Age of Extremes*, New York, 1994.

Hollohan, Francis and Baker, Melvin. *A Clear Head in Tempestuous Times*, St. John's, 1986.

Horwood, Harold. *Joey*, Toronto, 1989.

Innis, Harold. *The Cod Fisheries: The History of an International Economy*, Toronto, 1954.

Jackson, F. L. *Newfoundland in Canada*, St. John's, 1984.

Mackay, R. *Newfoundland: Economic, Diplomatic and Strategic Studies*, Toronto, 1946.

Macfarlane, David. *The Danger Tree*, Toronto, 1991.

MacPherson, C. B. *Democracy in Alberta: Social Credit and the Party System*, Toronto, 1953.

Martin, Cabot. *No Fish and Our Lives*, St. John's, 1992

McDonald, Ian. *To Each His Own, William Coaker and the Fishermen's Protective Union in Newfoundland Politics, 1908-1925*, St. John's, 1987.

Neary, Peter. *Newfoundland in the North Atlantic World, 1929-1949*, Montreal, 1988.

——. *The Political Economy of Newfoundland, 1929-1972*, Toronto, 1973.

——. *White Tie and Decorations*, Toronto, 1996.

Noel, S. J. *Politics in Newfoundland*, Toronto, 1970.

Prowse, D. J. *A History of Newfoundland*, London, 1895.

Sider, Gerald. *Culture and Class in Anthropolgy and History: A Newfoundland Illustration*, New York, 1986.

Smallwood, Joseph R. *Coaker of Newfoundland: The Man Who Led the Deep Sea Fishermen to Political Power*, London, 1927.

——. *The New Newfoundland*, New York, 1931.

——. *I Chose Canada*, Toronto, 1973.

Thompson, Frederic F. *The French Shore Problem in Newfoundland*, Toronto, 1961.

Thompson, John H. with Allen Seager. *Canada 1922-1939: Decades of Discord*, Toronto, 1985.

UNPUBLISHED THESES AND PAPERS

Baker, Melvin. "The Government of St. John's, Newfoundland, 1800-1921", PhD thesis, University of Western Ontario, 1980.

Chisolm, Jessie. "Hang Her Down: Strikes in St. John's, 1890-1914", paper, 1988.

Feltham, John. "The Development of the FPU in Newfoundland, 1908-1923", MA thesis, Memorial University of Newfoundland, 1959.

Greene, John. "The Influence of Religion in the Politics of Newfoundland, 1850-1861", MA thesis, Memorial University of Newfoundland, 1970.

Fenwick, Peter. "Witnesses to the Lord", paper, 1984.

Harvey, J. "The Framework of Industrial Society", paper, 1919.

Hart, Peter. "The Breakdown of Democracy in Newfoundland, 1931-1934", paper, 1987.

Hiller, James K. "A History of Newfoundland, 1874-1901", PhD thesis, Cambridge, 1971.

Kerr, Kenneth. "A Social Analysis of the Members of the House of Assembly, Executive Council and Legislative

Council for 1855-1914", MA thesis, Memorial University of Newfoundland, 1983.

Joy, John. "The Growth and Development of Trades and Manufacturing in St. John's, 1870-1914", MA thesis, Memorial University of Newfoundland, 1977.

McCorquodale, Susan. "Public Administration in Newfoundland During the Period of the Commission of Government: A Question of Political Development", PhD thesis, Queen's University, 1973.

McDonald, Ian. "William F. Coaker and the Fishermen's Protective Union in Newfoundland Politics, 1908-1925", PhD thesis, University of London, 1971.

McInnis, Peter. "Newfoundland Labour and World War I: The Emergence of the Newfoundland Industrial Workers' Association", MA thesis, Memorial University of Newfoundland, 1988.

Neis, Barbara. "A Sociological Analysis of the Factors Responsible for the Regional Distribution of the Fishermen's Protective Union of Newfoundland", MA thesis, Memorial University of Newfoundland, 1980.

O'Brien, Pat. "The Newfoundland Patriotic Association: The Administration of the War Effort, 1914-1918", MA thesis, Memorial University of Newfoundland, 1983.

Thistle, James. "The Election of 1932 and the Suspension of Democracy", paper, 1990.

Webb, Jeff. "Newfoundland's National Convention, 1946-1948", MA thesis, Memorial University of Newfoundland, 1987.

Crossroads Country

Malcolm MacLeod
ISBN 1-55081-144-4 / $19.95 (sc)
5" x 8" / 392 pp. (NF History Series)

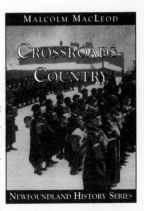

Crossroads Country is a collection of life stories of people who worked or studied at Memorial College before Confederation. It weaves together stories of friendships, kin networks, and lifetime connections into a fabric of Newfoundland culture of the 1930s and '40s. It examines the various ties that New-foundland enjoyed with Canada, the United States and Great Britain to form it into the culturally unique place that it is today.

MALCOLM MACLEOD

A native of Armdale (Halifax), Nova Scotia, Malcolm MacLeod is a graduate of Dalhousie, Toronto and University of Ottawa (Ph.D., 1974) who first stepped ashore on Newfoundland 30 years ago. He lives with his wife Heather in Chamberlains, Conception Bay South, close to other family members. He teaches history at Memorial University of Newfoundland, and is a past president of the Newfoundland Historical Society.

He has contributed to *The Canadian Encyclopedia; Colonial Wars of North America: An Encyclopedia; Dictionary of Canadian Biography* and *Encyclopedia of Newfoundland and Labrador;* and is the author of numerous scholarly articles in periodicals including *Acadiensis, Newfoundland Quarterly, Nova Scotia Historical Review, Ontario History* and *Canadian Historical Review. Crossroads Country* is his third major published work.